I0123749

The Human Factor in Mergers, Acquisitions, and Transformational Change

The Human Factor in Mergers, Acquisitions, and Transformational Change

Muhammad Rafique

BEP

BUSINESS EXPERT PRESS

Leader in applied, concise business books

The Human Factor in Mergers, Acquisitions, and Transformational Change

Copyright © Business Expert Press, LLC, 2022.

Cover design by Charlene Kronstedt

Interior design by Exeter Premedia Services Private Ltd., Chennai, India

All rights reserved. No part of this publication may be reproduced, stored in a retrieval system, or transmitted in any form or by any means—electronic, mechanical, photocopy, recording, or any other except for brief quotations, not to exceed 400 words, without the prior permission of the publisher.

First published in 2021 by
Business Expert Press, LLC
222 East 46th Street, New York, NY 10017
www.businessexpertpress.com

ISBN-13: 978-1-63742-145-1 (paperback)
ISBN-13: 978-1-63742-146-8 (e-book)

Business Expert Press Finance and Financial
Management Collection

Collection ISSN: 2331-0049 (print)
Collection ISSN: 2331-0057 (electronic)

First edition: 2021

10 9 8 7 6 5 4 3 2 1

Description

Mergers and Acquisitions have been used for many decades to improve efficiency, value generation, cost savings, and increasing market share. However, historically, 70 to 90 percent of these mergers and acquisitions fail or fail to achieve the holistic objectives. Over ambitious management, lack of strategic oversight, inaccurate valuation, unforeseen economic factors, and mishandling of integration obstacles generally lead to merger or acquisition failures. In this book, we focus on integration obstacles, specifically human emotions, and postmerger resource management.

Dedicated staff are an invaluable asset for any organization but when the uncertainty caused by potential change such as merger, acquisition, or restructuring creeps in, the performance is significantly impacted. Senior management focus on organizational challenges and staff feel neglected, under-valued, and ill-informed or even worse, misinformed. In some cases, experienced staff members leave the organization and the management is expected to deliver change with inexperienced and unmotivated staff, leading to laying the foundations of a failed merger.

This book offers: early warnings to business leaders; tried and tested strategies to keep staff onboard during all stages of organizational change; empathically addressing staff members' fears and emotional issues'; and a practical guide to integrate resources. This book is an adaptation of the doctoral thesis titled: 'The role of coaching and mentoring in transformational change, focusing on housing association mergers'. Anonymized real-life accounts of staff members working at various levels within the organizations as well as the experiences of external gurus, trainers, and coaches involved in delivering organizational change are included.

To aid organizational leaders tasked with delivering organizational change, case studies, exercises, and a unique "Coach's Corner" summarizing each preceding chapter and providing specific suggestions for leadership development are included from for profit as well as not for profit sectors. We believe that no such practical guide currently exists in the literature. The audience for our book includes business leaders, change agents, staff members facing organizational restructuring, business coaches, mentors, and ambitious managers considering transitioning into leadership positions.

Keywords

emotional sensibility during M&A; transformational change; merger process model; merger and acquisition failures; cultural compatibility; leadership development; cross-organizational mentoring; confidence coaching; staff integration

Contents

Testimonials

"All too often, we reduce Mergers and Acquisitions to financial transactions. (Muhammad) reminds us that there is a significant human element in every M&A story; one that needs to be well understood and managed. Using his double background in finance and coaching, he brings these—often separate—worlds together, to provide a pragmatic approach to support the success of such major transformational events."—**Dr. Hany Shoukry, Group Director, Sky UK**

"There is always an emotional response when organisations merge, even when the driving factor is financial so that jobs can be retained. However, the employee's responses are not always addressed effectively and can sometimes be detrimental to the whole process. Muhammad addresses the missing link here and explores how coaching and mentoring can be used to support employees as they transition through organisational mergers. This is such an important element which needs to be better understood and applied, if organisations are going to thrive and succeed."—**Dr. Tina Salter, Senior Lecturer, University of Bedfordshire**

"This book is an indispensable resource for anyone involved in dynamics of transformational change. It provides a unique in-depth perspective on the processes within mergers and acquisitions as being affected by intricate essence of human behavior. The lessons learned and explicated by this guide would help practitioners to deconstruct and master the complex mechanics of organizational change."—**Dr. Alex Avramenko, Professor of Business and Management, Abertay University, UK**

CHAPTER 1

Introduction

Merger and acquisition failures are established phenomena. The failure rates vary according to some analysts, scholars, and researchers. Statistics show that approximately 50 percent of all mergers and acquisitions fail to achieve the intended results (William 2005). The failure rate of merged firms in creating value and meeting their desired financial or strategic objectives is even higher. Marks and Mirvis (2010) point out that roughly 70 to 75 percent of corporate partnerships failed, whereas the failure rate as per Christensen et al. (2011) is 80 to 90 percent. Therefore, statistically every other merger is doomed for failure.

Consistent merger failures have provided scholars with abundance of data and different theories have been developed. Seo and Hill (2005) identify six theories to explain the problems in managing mergers and acquisitions: anxiety theory, social identity theory, acculturation theory, role conflict theory, job characteristic theory, and organizational justice theory. In addition to the evidence-based academic literature, there are various practical guides, models, and toolkits developed by practitioners, gurus, and consultants to help and support the senior management teams involved in the merger process. This book adds to the body of academic and practitioners' literature by highlighting the impact of human emotions on the success and failure of a merger. Historically, lessons from merger failures have not been learnt and same mistakes have been repeated time and again in various settings.

If senior executives responsible for initiating and managing mergers are not changing their strategies in the presence of all the resources available to them, what is the point of another book? This is a genuine question. The purpose of this book is not to offer a tick box flow chart, step by step guide or a management mantra for merger success. Instead, the importance of human factors in the management of mergers is discussed with specific reference to the theories that highlight staff-related problems in the management of mergers. Workplace learning theories relating to the desirability and acceptability of the need for transformational changes are also reviewed.

Mergers, acquisitions, transformational change, and organizational change are the terms used interchangeably in practice and are reflected so in this book. Since mergers and acquisitions can readily change the nature and character of the organizations in question, they can be usefully conceived as a form of organizational transformation (Buono and Bowditch 2003). The term "transformation" appears to be freely used in the organizational change literature to describe, for instance: a change in the shape, structure, and nature of something (Tosey and Robinson 2002); downsizing and de-layering (Worral et al. 1998); an infrequent, rapid and large change (Jarrett 2003); a change in dominant ideologies, cultural systems of meaning and power relations in an organization (Pettigrew 1987); and a revolutionary change, affecting the whole organization at once (Greenwood and Hinings 1996).

All mergers, acquisitions, and transformational change programs are designed to create and consolidate shareholders value. No chief executive officer has come forward and said that the merger or acquisition will adversely affect the customers and clients. Conversely, all mergers and acquisitions are propagated as in the best interest of customers, by offering complementary products and services; value for money as some of the savings are passed on to customers, provision of consistently high-quality service to customers. In reality, the uncertainty caused by the change adversely affects frontline staff who are the face of the company and point of contact for the customers. This adds to the pressure on executives to do something quickly to fix the problem.

The potential causes of merger failure identified in the literature, include: agency problems, optimism, and conflicting cultural values between the employees in the two merged firms. Mergers and acquisitions lead to large-scale changes to the organizational structure and result in affecting core systems, traditional ways of working, and shift in organizational identity and values. When an organization acquires or merges with its fierce rival, the attitude of new comrades does not become friendly and collegial at once. Organizations have unique cultures and reconciling them is an extremely difficult task. Expecting a large number of staff to forget their previous organizational culture and switch to a new one result in stress, anxiety, and reduced productivity. Many change initiators lack the emotional intelligence to appreciate the power of human emotions and do not factor these emotions in their calculations. Cultural incompatibility has been commonly associated with merger failures by a number of scholars, including Buono and Bowditch (2003), Cartwright et al. (2007), and Marks and Mirvis (2010). Human factors, such as acceptance of and readiness for change at the individual level, conflict of interest, and cultural incompatibility, are the key attributes of the success or failure of a merger or transformational change.

In her study of the merger between two higher education institutions, Arthur (2010) asserted that mergers represent a complex change. Lam (2010) acknowledges resistance to change because of fear or uncertainty and complexity, especially with the loss of jobs arising from mergers between organizations. He suggests that change management should include counseling, support, and training. Kiefer (2002, 39) describes organizational changes, especially mergers as "emotive events," in which emotions emerge from change processes and are inseparably linked with organizational action. In her analysis of the merger and organizational change literature, Kiefer put (negative) emotions into three groups: (1) stress, fear, anxiety, and insecurity because of the uncertainty; (2) anger and loss of trust following staff redundancies; and (3) resistance to change, which Kiefer (2002, 41) classed as "irrational emotions" due to a lack of understanding of the implications of change. She warns against the stereotypical negativity attached to emotions during change and argues that people can experience a range of positive and negative emotions. The positive emotions noted by Kiefer (2002) include curiosity, enthusiasm, pride, security, trust, and hope.

Impact of positive emotions on the success of a merger or acquisition has not been quantified in literature. The beneficiaries of a merger or an acquisition, who enjoy positive emotions can be the staff and executives receiving golden goodbyes, talent recognition for handling complex change in a professional manner, leadership training and development, and promotion under the new structure. According to a conservative estimate, 20 percent of staff risk losing their jobs following the merger. Therefore, the number of staff positively affected by the change is far less than the ones who are not the winners and beneficiaries.

Regardless of their standing within an organization, most people do not like change. If the senior management tries to inject some false positivity to win over people or to calm their nerves, by slogans, such as "business as usual," "this challenge will make us strong," "we have a wonderful future ahead" …, they lose the credibility more quickly than they imagine. When the emotions are already high, staff can see change in front of their eyes, they can sense fear of unknown in the air, they get further infuriated when senior management insults their intelligence.

Even if the need for change is identified and agreed upon, it is almost impossible to have a homogeneous approach to the process, pace, and practical implications of change. Cinite et al. (2009), Jansson (2013), and Kuntz and Gomes (2012) observed that an organization is not considered ready for change by the employees in cases where the employees are not provided with a vision for change, the reasons behind the change, or the expected outcomes and benefits of the transformational change.

For an organizational change to succeed, individuals need a proper vision and ideas about outcomes, and have to learn and develop new behaviors to comply with change requirements. Just having a vision does not make one a visionary leader. Having the competence, capacity, and compassion to make everyone in the organization to share that vision and to work cohesively to achieve the common goal is the hallmark of a visionary leader.

Mergers and acquisitions fail because of people. Due diligence reports focus on the monetary aspects of the merger, detailing cost savings from making staff redundant from the overlap activities or streamlining operations. There is no mechanism in due diligence reports for the identification and retention of talented staff. Having witnessed and experienced several mergers, acquisitions, and other transformational change exercises, it can be said with a degree of certainty that in the first instance, management invites voluntary severance applications to keep the compulsory redundancies to a minimum. Senior staff members with a wealth of experience are the first ones to leave generally. Ironically this pleases senior executives because the cost reduction box is being ticked, as senior people leaving the organization are normally on high salaries. The next group of people to leave are the ambitious ones who see uncertainty created by the change detrimental to their career ambitions and personal objectives.

That again pleases senior executives because their trusted cronies convince senior executives that if these people do not share the vision and are not comfortable working under your leadership, it is better that they are leaving. Nobody realizes that the experienced and ambitious staff are an important asset and have contributed to make this organization an attractive merger or acquisition target. In many cases, the organizations are left with staff who lack experience or ambition or even both. Now the business leaders have to deliver the promises made before the merger with this workforce. If the premerger cultural audits were not conducted and the organizational cultures clash then it is doomed for failure, because you are dealing with people who are unwilling or unable to change. This results in another statistic, another addition to the ever growing infamous hall of failed mergers.

Time-line model provided in this book focuses on the emotional and behavioral aspects of business leaders, senior managers, operational, and frontline staff during four distinct phases of a merger or an acquisition. The four phases are (1) Before Merger: cultural compatibility, organizational structures, and financial systems of the potential merger partners or acquisition targets are scrutinized before entering an agreement, (2) Premerger: senior and operational management are designated clear responsibilities and additional training provided to handle the change effectively and compassionately, (3) During merger: all staff members are kept informed about the developments, changes to the job roles, revised organizational structure communicated in a frank and honest manner, and (4) Postmerger: new organizational culture and shared identities are developed while respecting and retaining former organizational identities, the concept of identity within an identity is introduced.

By reading, considering, contemplating, and applying the model, business leaders, change agents, coaching and mentoring practitioners can tailor their services to the needs of the organizations anticipating a transformational change.

CHAPTER 2

Rear-View Mirror Perspective

In this chapter, some recent and some historic failed mergers are critically analyzed, mistakes made by those responsible for delivering change, miscalculations of the strategists, and other factors contributing to the unintended results are scrutinized with the benefit of hindsight with a view to learn from others' mistakes.

Failed to Complete Mergers

Before discussing the mergers and acquisitions that failed soon after or a few years after the actual merger, let us cast an eye on the mergers and acquisitions that were stopped in their tracks. This is not the case where one firm showed interest in merging with or acquiring another firm. Not even the case where after mutual interest, the expectations of one firm were not met and the negotiations failed. This is the case, where it was public knowledge that the merger was eminent but it did not happen. One must view each merger on its own merits but there are certain common factors that can lead to "failed to complete" mergers. Some of the factors include (1) strong reaction from investors, (2) strong reaction from government, and (3) questionable merger motives.

Strong Reaction From Investors

If the investors view the potential merger as value destruction, some start selling their stocks in the firms that results in reduced share price. This signals the markets that the deal is not in the best interest of the investors. In 2019, a potential merger between Altria and Philip Morris was called off because of the strong reaction from investors.

Philip Morris International (PMI) describes themselves as a leading international tobacco company and claim to have built world's most successful cigarette company with the world's most popular and iconic brands, including Marlboro, Merit, Parliament, Virginia Slims, and Benson & Hedges.

In 2017, PMI officially laid out its vision for a "smoke-free" future and plan to switch smokers to PMI's new range of cigarette alternatives, which PMI claim would improve public health. They launched the "Unsmoke Your World" campaign and pledged to stop selling cigarettes in the UK by 2030. PMI are developing e-cigarettes into next generation of e-vapor technology. Their heated tobacco system IQOS (I Quit Ordinary Smoking) has been launched in many markets around the world.

Altria Group Inc. is an American corporation and one of the world's largest producers and marketers of tobacco, cigarettes, and related products. They describe the tobacco companies in the group as "undisputed market leaders in the U.S. tobacco industry for decades." Altria group owns Philip Morris USA, Smokeless Tobacco Company, John Middleton, 80 percent interest in Helix Innovations, the manufacturers of oral tobacco-derived nicotine pouch products, and 35 percent ownership of JUUL Labs Inc., e-vapor company.

Philip Morris was spun off from Altria Group in 2008, but decided to merge again in 2019. However, as banning of flavored e-cigarettes was being considered by Food and Drug Administration (FDA), the merger was called off. The uncertainty caused by further regulation and shareholders reaction had a negative impact on the share price. The news of merger cancellation resulted in instant increase in share price.

Strong Reaction From Government

If the government views the merger to be not in the public interest, a clear message is sent to the merging firms and to avoid unintended legal proceedings, the merger is abandoned.

MCI Worldcom and Sprint

In 1999, MCI Worldcom and Sprint were close to merging when the U.S. Department of Justice and European Commission prohibited the merger on competition grounds and the U.S. Department of Justice filed a lawsuit against the transaction. The proposed $115 billion acquisition of Sprint by MCI Worldcom would have been the biggest corporate combination in the history at that time.

On October 04, 1999, MCI WorldCom and Sprint signed an agreement and plan of merger under which Sprint stock will be exchanged for MCI WorldCom stock. Sprint will be merged into MCI WorldCom and will lose its separate corporation existence while MCI WorldCom will continue as the surviving corporation.

European Commission's report described both MCI WorldCom and Sprint as global communications companies. MCI WorldCom provides a wide range of telecommunications services to businesses and consumers, including facilities-based local, long distance and international freephone, calling card, debit card, and Internet services. Sprint provides in the U.S. local, long-distance, and wireless communications and Internet services. Sprints activities in Europe were (until Sprints withdrawal from its participation in Global One, a joint venture with Deutsche Telekom and France Telecom) conducted through Global One.

Pfizer and AstraZeneca

Proposed merger of Pfizer and AstraZeneca started with a promise of "win–win" situation for all, but was abandoned following interest from the UK politicians. Pfizer Inc. is an American multinational pharmaceutical corporation and one of the world's largest pharmaceutical companies with its headquarters in New York city, United States. Astra Zeneca PLC is a British Swedish multinational pharmaceutical and biopharmaceutical company with its global headquarters in Cambridge, UK.

Sequence of events make this proposed merger an interesting read. In November 2013, Ian Read, Chief Executive Officer (CEO) of Pfizer contacted Leif Johansson, chairman of AstraZeneca to discuss a potential merger. Both business leaders agreed to meet in early 2014. On January 05, 2014, high-level talks between the senior management of both companies were held in New York in which Pfizer proposed paying £46.61 per AstraZeneca share, valuing the company at £58 billion. This offer was declined by AstraZeneca as it undervalued the company.

On April 26, 2014, Ian Read contacted Leif Johansson again to restart the merger talks but did not present any concrete attractive proposal and the board of AstraZeneca refused to discuss the merger. On the same day, senior management of Pfizer sold significant number of their shares in Pfizer. Ian Read sold $10.6 million in shares and Frank D'Amelio, Chief Finance Officer of Pfizer, sold $8.9 million in shares, according to Regulatory filing May 16, 2014.

Going back to the timeline, after April 26, 2014 refusal of Astra Zeneca board to discuss the merger, Pfizer made public announcement about their interest in AstraZeneca on April 28, 2014, two days after offloading significant shareholding in Pfizer.

On May 02, 2014, Pfizer made an increased indictive offer of £50 per share valuing AstraZeneca at £63 billion. Pfizer also wrote to the UK Prime Minister David Cameron pledging to keep 20 percent of the merged company's research workforce in Cambridge, UK for at least five years and to base the company's European operations in the UK. In their April 28, 2014 announcement, Pfizer had declared to move its domicile to the UK to shield its non-U.S. earnings from the U.S. taxes.

On May 04, 2014, Ed Milliband, leader of the opposition, increased the political pressure by raising the national interest issue and called for the independent assessment of the takeover.

On May 07, 2014, David Cameron told the UK parliament that he wants stronger assurance from Pfizer about potential job losses and cuts to the UK science research.

On May 08, 2014, Lord Sainsbury, former science minister, accused Pfizer of being an asset stripper and called for the proposed takeover to be blocked, as in his view, Pfizer wanted to "dismember" an important British company.

On May 13, 2014, Ian Read and AstraZeneca Chief Executive Pascal Soriot separately appeared in front of the UK Business, Innovation, and Skills committee where Soriot warned that the merger could endanger lives by delaying the development of important drugs. Whereas, in his representation, Ian Read dismissed the warning as "red herring" but did accept that the merger would result in reduced research spending and job losses.

On May 14, 2014, Read and Soriot appeared in parliament again, this time before the science and technology committee. Read admitted there would be fewer scientists in the combined company than at present but insisted that Pfizer would honor its legally binging commitments to UK investment. But Soriot said that the research could be set back if his scientists leave the company because they oppose the merger.

On May 15, 2014, the chair of the science select committee, Andrew Miller, wrote to the science minister David Willetts expressing his growing concerns about Pfizer's £63 billion takeover approach to AstraZeneca, adding to the overwhelming sense of unease within Britain's science community.

On May 16, 2014, shadow business secretary, Chuka Umunna, threatened to block the proposed £63 billion takeover of AstraZeneca by Pfizer if his party win the general election.

On May18, 2014, Pfizer made a new offer of £55 per share, valuing AstraZeneca at £69 billion to put pressure on AstraZeneca's board to enter negotiations with Pfizer. This bid was also rejected.

AstraZeneca chairman Leif Johansson said that Pfizer "failed to make a compelling strategic, business or value" case. In his interview to the BBC, David Cameron said that he would remain neutral about AstraZeneca's rejection of the bid from Pfizer, although government officials are still involved in talks with both companies. He further added, "the government quite rightly should be neutral on this. What we should do, though, is always be engaged with both companies, as we have been, to try and make sure that whatever the outcome, British science, British jobs, British manufacturing get proper and deserved attention."

Questionable Merger Motives

In 1999, Telecom Italia, then the largest telecommunications company in Italy, was fighting off a hostile takeover bid from Olivetti, an Italian company specializing in the electronic equipment, that is smart phones, computers, printers, tablets, and calculators. The management of Telecom Italia started negotiating a merger deal with Deutsche Telecom, a German telecommunications company, to fend off Olivetti interest. Deutsche Telekom was one of the largest telecommunications providers in Europe and it was a proposed acquisition of Telecom Italia. However, both companies insisted that it was a merger of equals even though Deutsche

Telekom would have approximately 55 percent control. Had this $80 billion merger succeeded, the merged company would become the second largest telecommunications company in the world. Large-scale deals like this do require thorough due diligence, clearance from the regulatory authorities, and in this situation approval from respective governments. Because of the amount of time being taken to finalize the deal, Olivetti managed to sway key Telecom Italia shareholders and obtained control of 51 percent of shares in Telecom Italia. When merger negotiations prolong and financial situation of both parties gain public interest, in some cases, another interested party can take advantage of the situation and the proposed merger talks collapse prematurely.

Failed to complete mergers and acquisitions cause reputational damage to the senior management of both companies. Time and energy used in pursuing a deal that did not conclude in company's benefit can be seen as management's failure to foresee potential hurdles and inability to overcome them. Time and money spent on initial consultation and due diligence process is an issue as well.

For a merger or an acquisition to be a good deal for shareholders, it has to go through the premerger screening and scrutiny. If the management proceeds with a deal only because they initially thought it to be beneficial for the shareholders but the due diligence reports contradicted that perception, it would be value destruction for the shareholders. For finalizing a merger, the firms must consider: (1) strategic fit, (2) realistic postmerger synergies, (3) compatibility of organizational cultures, (4) potential regulatory issues and cost and time frame for their resolution, (5) infrastructure adaptability, (6) ability to retain talent, and (7) capacity to deliver postmerger integration.

Failed Mergers

Having seen some examples of mergers that failed to complete, lets' move on to mergers that passed the hurdle of completion but failed to deliver the promised postmerger results. A failed merger is the one where merged organizations do not achieve their set objectives.

Human attributes can decide the success or failure of a merger. Anticipated results, whether it is profit maximization, cost savings, increased efficiencies, or installing a new business model, can only be achieved if the staff contributing to achieve these results are onboard. In a merger, corporate mission of all merger partners have to be the unanimously agreed one. Regardless of the fact whether, before the merger, the organizations' individual corporate missions were complementary or contradictory. After the merger, the staff bring with them organizational culture, who knows how much effort and energy had been put to develop and instill that organizational culture. In addition to the organizational culture, staff also bring their own personalities, ambitions, behavioral traits, and preferred working style. There is a lot that staff and management are required to unlearn before starting on learning new ways of working after the merger. To adapt to a new corporate mission and to adapt instantly to achieve that is very difficult. Therefore, many newly merged organizations fail to achieve their objectives. Cutting costs and achieving efficiency saving targets by making excess staff redundant are easy. What is not easy, is to develop the remainder staff into an efficient, productive, and cohesive unit and to achieve revenue generation targets.

Kison Patel, the CEO of DealRoom, identified 10 common reasons why mergers and acquisitions fail. These reasons include: (1) overpayment to seal the deal, (2) overestimating synergies, (3) insufficient due diligence, (4) misunderstanding the target company, (5) lack of a strategic plan, (6) lack of cultural fit, (7) overextending resources, (8) wrong time in industry cycle, (9) external factors, and (10) lack of management involvement.

Lets' have a look at some failed mergers that have almost achieved the legendary folklores status.

AOL–Time Warner

In their case study, Malone and Turner (2010) state that initially stock market reacted positively to the announcement of the merger between AOL and Time Warner. The market value of AOL was $164 billion and the market value of Time Warner $97 billion, making the total value of these companies before merger of $261 billion. However, the combined value after the merger was estimated at $361 billion, based on the $110 per share value assigned to the Time Warner shares in the merger agreement. Hence, the postmerger value increase of $100 billion, which was due to the potential advantages from synergies in operations, customer reach, and technological infrastructure. Instead, the merger yielded to $99 billion net loss in 2002, the biggest loss ever, the company reported $45 billion write down in 2003, and then a $100 billion yearly loss. Around 2009, Time Warner completely withdrew from the Internet and back into its own entity, so after seven years the two companies were unable to realize the merger synergies.

On May 28, 2009 Time Warner Inc. announced that it would spin off AOL; the news came as no surprise, according to Malone and Turner (2010). They further stated that, the day Time Warner announced the AOL spinoff, Steve Case, no longer with Time Warner, posted a Twitter entry that said, "Thomas Edison: 'Vision without execution is hallucination'—pretty much sums up AOL/TW—failure of leadership (myself included)."

Tim Arango, in the "In Retrospect" section of *The New York Times*, on January 10, 2010 wrote, "Today the combined value of the companies (AOL and Time Warner), which have been separated, is about one-seventh of their worth on the day of merger." He described the initial merger transaction "worst in history'" in which "some of the brightest minds in technology and media collaborated to produce a deal now regarded by many as a colossal mistake." It is widely reported that the deal was sealed at a dinner at Stephen Case's house between Gerald Levin Chief Executive of Time Warner and Stephen Case cofounder of AOL. Tim Arango wrote, "over a weekend, the two sides conducted due diligence, with teams of lawyers camped out in two law offices in Manhattan."

Some of the factors identified by Kishon Patel contributed to the failure of AOL–Time Warner merger, including (1) overestimating synergies, (2) insufficient due diligence, (3) wrong time in industry cycle, (4) lack of management involvement, and (5) lack of cultural fit.

Factors (1) and (2) are clear from Tim Arango's observations above. Let's have a brief look at the remaining three factors. Timing of the AOL–Time Warner merger was not ideal.

Timing of the merger deal between AOL and Time Warner turned out to be a factor in the failure. The intention was to bring together the leading Internet company AOL and leading media company Time

Warner together to create a new company with the potential to lead in the new century. However, according to some analysts, the year 2000 was not a good time for media firms to merge. The media industry was about to undergo the biggest shake-up in its history. At the same time, the dot-com bubble burst. According to Malone and Turner (2010), when the Internet bubble burst, it took down nearly any and all companies that had participated in the earlier Internet craze; AOL–Time Warner was no exception.

Lack of management involvement was another key factor in the AOL and Time Warner merger failure. Staff of both merging firms were kept in the dark about the merger. They found out on the day of merger through the media. Senior executives and directors who were to be responsible to make the merger a success, weren't informed never mind being consulted prior to the merger. Tim Arango wrote that the weekend before January 10, 2000, when the lawyers were finalizing due diligence, Gerald Levin and Stephen Case began notifying their senior executives. Don Logan, then head of Time Inc., and Ted Leonsis, division president of the AOL, were notified of the merger at that weekend, whereas many executives found out about the deal the day of announcement in a conference call at 08:00 a.m.

Lack of cultural fit also contributed to the AOL and Time Warner merger failure. As noted above, financial due diligence was rushed at the last minute, there is no evidence of any effort to assess the cultural compatibility of the merging firms. It is argued that the failure of AOL–Time Warner merger was highly attributed to the variation in the organizations culture. Malone and Turner (2010) note that the two companies had very different corporate cultures and there was serious friction after the merger between AOL executives and employees and Time Warner executives and employees. According to some analysts, AOL had arrogant and aggressive employees while Time Warner had corporate and staid employees and even though the merging sounded strategically compelling, the two companies could not manage the merger due to cultural variation.

Sprint—Nextel

In 2005, Sprint and Nextel merged to form Sprint Nextel, the third biggest telecommunications network in the United States. This was dubbed as the merger of equals and on surface it appeared so. Gary Forsee, the CEO and Chairman of Sprint, became the CEO of the merged company, while Timothy Donahue, Nextel CEO, became the chairman of Sprint Nextel. The board of directors was split equally and six directors from Sprint and six from Nextel were appointed to the board of Sprint Nextel. Some analysts argue that it wasn't a merger of equals but Sprint acquired 100 percent of Nextel's common shares. Celiktas et al. (2016) assert that Gary Forsee was the primary influencer of the deal. He was motivated to capitalize on each company's competitive advantage. The companies' complementary products and services were seen as a persuasive argument for the merger and Nextel CEO, Timothy Donahue could not agree more.

In a conference call with the press, Donahue said, "This new, powerhouse company has the spectrum, infrastructure, distribution, and superb and differentiated product portfolio that will drive our continued success."

Celiktas et al. (2016) identified the following strategic and financial benefits of this merger:

- Gain operating efficiencies that neither company could achieve on its own.
- Increase revenue by cross-selling products.
- Accelerate pace of bringing new products to market.
- Reduce capital spending by leveraging existing networks and cell sites.
- Reduce expenses from consolidated customer care, billing, marketing, and general expenses.

The merger that combined the third and fifth wireless carriers with combined 40 million customers, the potential benefits mentioned above should be realistically achievable. Sprint was a leader in wireless data communications and Nextel was the walkie-talkie service pioneer with business customers as their basic customer base. However, the merger spectacularly failed. Because of the unique situation of this merger, 10 common reasons for merger failure noted by Kison Patel don't appropriately comprehend the situation. Following three factors directly attributed to the failure of

Sprint Nextel merger: (1) lack of cultural audit, premerger, (2) infrastructure incompatibility, and (3) lack of postmerger integration.

Organizational cultures of Sprint and Nextel were very different. Sprint's organizational culture was bureaucratic, planning was centralized, and decisions were made by the top management. In contrast, Nextel boasted on entrepreneurial spirit and delegated decision making. They focused on creativity for the sake of innovation and vision, according to Celiktas et al. (2016). This diversion in organizational cultures was not appreciated and its impact on postmerger integration was not taken into consideration and foreseen by the architects of this merger. On November 24, 2007, Kim Hart, wrote in The Washington Post, "Two sharply different corporate cultures have resulted in clashes in everything from advertising strategies to cell phone technologies, preventing Sprint Nextel from becoming the merger of equals envisioned." The cultural differences led to disagreements and ended up with both groups mistrusting each other. Efforts were made to minimize the tension and to inject harmonization by employing external consultants but this strategy was not very successful because of the trust deficit.

Infrastructure incompatibility was another hurdle in achieving postmerger efficiency, additional revenue from cross-selling, and to integrate two networks. One of the merger motives was to exploit the complementary aspects of both companies by establishing interoperability across the combined infrastructure, for example, to extend Nextel's push-to-talk services to all of the Sprint Nextel customers. Gary Forsee boasted about creating more opportunities for customers, "We have proven market differentiators like push-to-talk, highly efficient Code Division Multiple Access (CDMA) technologies, advanced high speed data capabilities and wireless business solutions that are being delivered on the market today, not just promises for the future." However, he failed to appreciate the incompatibility of the network infrastructure, as Nextel phones could not be used in Sprint network system and Sprint phones could not be used in Nextel network system. This infrastructure incompatibility was something that could not be resolved in a short period of time or by the management effort, according to Yamini Verma (2019). This was a variation in the technology and thus, it was hard to integrate the two networks. The solution could have only been based on foregoing one form of network to another, or creating a whole different network, which simply meant losing customers from either the foregone company network or both in case a new network formed could not accommodate the two different phones. Therefore, incompatible infrastructure that lacked flexibility to allow efficient and cost-effective integration was one of the core reasons for this merger failure.

Dual Headquarters

Lack of postmerger staff integration was another factor that contributed to the Sprint Nextel merger failure. Before the merger, Nextel's headquarter was in Reston, VA, while Sprint was headquartered in Overland Park, KS. To avoid relocation-related disruption and anxiety to the affected staff and their families, the company decided to opt for dual headquarters. The board of directors voted to utilize Nextel's Reston base as Sprint Nextel Executive headquarter and Sprint's Overland park as Operational headquarter. Kim Hart (2007) noted that at one point a corporate jet shuttled between the two headquarters at least once a day. No matter how well-intended was the decision to minimize relocation, this certainly prolonged postmerger integration. Having executive and operational headquarters half a country apart does not foster collegiality and camaraderie needed to make the merger a success.

"Never should have happened," wrote Yamini Verma, wrote in Inventiva (2019) about the merger of Sprint and Nextel. She concluded, "The acquisition of Sprint and Nextel could be ascertained as one of the prominent examples to quote about how the amalgamation of two different organisations of different work culture and dissimilar integration interest can lead to crucial the success of organisation and subsequent failure. Had they have given priority to the corporate structuring things might have worked well for them." This eventful $35 billion merger ended in 2013 after the shutdown of Nextel network.

Bank of America—Countrywide

The acquisition of Countrywide Financial Corporation by the Bank of America turned out to be the story of a toxic acquisition. In 2006,

Countrywide financed 20 percent of all mortgages in the United States, at a value of about 3.5 percent of the United States GDP, a proportion greater than any other single mortgage lender. Countrywide acquired the market share by getting involved in questionable and in some cases, illegal practices, including applying the most flexible lending criteria permitted, discriminating against Black and Hispanic borrowers, misleading the bond issuers about the quality of mortgage packages, and fraud.

With the looming collapse of subprime mortgages, Angelo Mozilo, the CEO of Countrywide, was actively looking to diversify, to establish and strengthen other divisions, such as capital markets division. In 2007, he contacted Jimmy Dunne, the CEO of Sandler O'Neil and Partners, a small Wall Street investment bank, with a view to explore joint working arrangements. However, this proposition did not go very far, after reviewing Countrywide's financial records and meeting up with the senior executives, Dunne decided not to proceed. He was uncomfortable with the business model and senior management's approach to risk. In an interview to Connie Bruck (2009), Dunne explained his decision, "These guys were true believers … I was afraid of that, where was the doubting Thomas?"

In 2017, Wall Street buyers abandoned most mortgage-backed securities, including the ones offered by Countrywide. This pulled the rug from under their feet. Angelo Mozilo pleaded with his creditors to continue funding the short-term debt, known as commercial paper. Countrywide had used this facility to finance many of its loans (Connie Bruck 2009); however, on this occasion, this request was refused. In desperation, Countrywide borrowed $11.5 billion under pre-established lines of credit from 40 banks.

In August 2007, Bank of America announced a $2 billion repurchase agreement for Countrywide Financial. This purchase of preferred stock was arranged to provide a return on investment of 7.25 percent per annum and provided the option to purchase common stock at a price of $18 per share.

In January 2008, Bank of America announced that it would buy Countrywide for $4.1 billion. Bank of America thought it had a bargain (Dan Fitzpatrick, 2012). In reality, Bank of America was the sole prospective buyer, and it was offering to pay just over four billion dollars to acquire more than a thousand Countrywide offices and a loan portfolio of about $1.5 trillion and Mozilo was determined to seal the deal. Kenneth Lewis, Bank of America's then-chief executive, found the strategic temptation too hard to resist and overlooked the fact that in March 2008, Federal Bureau of Investigation had opened an investigation against Countrywide for possible fraud relating to home loans and mortgages.

At a time when Angelo Mozilo, the CEO of Countrywide, was forced to choose between bankruptcy and being acquired by Bank of America, according to Bruck (2009), Kenneth Lewis had the option to walk away from the deal, but he didn't. By 2012, the decision to acquire Countrywide has costed the Bank of America over $40 billion in real-estate losses, legal expenses, and settlements with state and federal agencies according to people close to the bank, writes Fitzpatrick (2012). Kenneth Lewis retired at the end of 2009, but Bank of America kept paying for years after his departure, for a deal that Kenneth Lewis classed as "a rare opportunity." Before discussing the role of Kenneth Lewis further, these are some of the financial penalties and charges Bank of America had to pay for Countrywide's decisions before the acquisition.

In June 2010, Bank of America agreed to pay $108 million to settle federal charges that Countrywide's loan-servicing operations had deceived homeowners who were behind on their payments into paying wildly inflated fees.

In May 2011, Bank of America reached a $20 million settlement of Justice Department charges that Countrywide had wrongfully foreclosed on active duty members of the armed forces without first obtaining required court orders.

In December 2011, Bank of America agreed to pay $335 million to settle charges that Countrywide had discriminated against minority customers.

In 2010, Angelo Mozilo was ordered to pay $22.5 million penalty to settle Securities and Exchange Commission charges for misleading investors.

Kenneth Lewis, in a company statement, justified his decision to acquire Countrywide, despite knowing the level of risk and potential legal issues. He said, "Countrywide presents a rare opportunity for Bank of America to add what we believe is the best domestic mortgage platform at an attractive price and to affirm our position as the nation's premier lender to consumers. We are aware of the issues within the housing and mortgage industries. The transaction reflects those challenges." This attitude gives rise to a number of questions, including was it an ego-filled mistake or a rational decision? Did the due diligence reports not capture the potential risks or the preparers of these reports could not afford to go against Lewis's wishes? Was Lewis overconfident or ignorant?

Mergers and acquisitions can fail for many reasons. One of the prominent reasons that comes out of the cases discussed earlier is the role of chief executive officers of the organizations involved in the merger or acquisition. Empire building egoist attitude, inability to engage with staff, insecurity to become answerable, arrogance to side-line doubters, lacking foresight, failing to delegate, failing to communicate ideas or intentions to the senior colleagues, and lacking self-awareness appear to be the personality traits of the business leaders involved in the aforementioned mergers. The corporate culture, stakeholder pressures, personal ambitions, and the killer instinct of some business leaders over power their capacities of: self-reflection, empathy, humiliation, and vulnerability that make us humane. In the next chapters, we discuss how coaches and mentors can help senior business leaders.

CHAPTER 3

Importance of Understanding and Being Responsive to Emotions

Change affects human beings asynchronously. Staff members affected by the same transformational change can have a range of emotions including anger, anxiety, confusion, empathetic pain, entrancement, fear, and triumph. This chapter highlights possible reasons for resisting change, importance of creating a trusting environment, creating a safe space for staff to express their concerns, and business leaders as co-travelers in the emotional roller coaster.

This chapter starts with an explanation of transformation change and how it is presented in the academic and practitioners' literature. The human factors determining the acceptance or rejection of transformational change are outlined. Some commonly known transformational change models are critically analyzed with a view to assess the usefulness of such models in the transformational change environment. Then theoretical bases and utilization of coaching and mentoring to deal with stress and anxiety caused by transformational change are included along with transformative learning, resulting from these interventions.

Transformational Change

Transformational change is the emergence of an entirely new state prompted by a shift in what is considered possible or necessary which results in a profoundly different structure, culture, or level of performance, according to Dougall et al. (2018). Since mergers and acquisitions can readily change the nature and character of the organizations, they can be usefully conceived as a form of organizational transformation

(Buono and Bowditch 2003). The term "transformation" is freely used in the organizational change literature to describe, for instance: a change in the shape, structure, and nature of something; downsizing and de-layering; an infrequent, rapid, and large change; a change in dominant ideologies, cultural systems of meaning, and power relations in an organization; and a revolutionary change, affecting the whole organization at once.

Transformation is commonly related to organizational change, and organizations are under intense pressure to change, to be more efficient, compete for business, and undertake complex streamlining processes as many organizations are moving into an uncertain future and have no option but to significantly redesign their business model. Therefore, transformational change is unavoidable in many organizations operating in a turbulent environment. The organizational change literature describes transformational change as a necessity for survival and the only alternative to corporate oblivion.

Mergers represent a complex change. There is ever increasing pressure on organizations to undergo change (Issah 2018) to survive and maintain their relevance. Lam (2010) acknowledges resistance to change because of fear or uncertainty and complexity, especially with the loss of a job arising from mergers between organizations. Emotions are critical determinants of employee attitudes and behaviors in mergers and acquisitions (Sarala et al. 2019). Resistance by employees and other stakeholders may slow down the postmerger integration process (Renneboog and Vansteenkiste 2019). Lam (2010) suggests that change management should include counseling, support, and training.

Kiefer (2002) describes organizational changes, especially mergers as "emotive events," in which emotions emerge from change processes and are inseparably linked with organizational action (p. 39). In her analysis of the merger and organizational change literature, Kiefer put (negative) emotions into three groups: (1) stress, fear, anxiety, and insecurity because of the uncertainty; (2) anger and loss of trust following staff redundancies; and (3) resistance to change, which Kiefer (2002, 41) classed as "irrational emotions" due to a lack of understanding of the implications of change. She warns against the stereotypical negativity attached to emotions during change and argues that people can experience a range of positive and negative emotions. The positive emotions noted by Kiefer

(2002) include: curiosity, enthusiasm, pride, security, trust, and hope. In their study, De Keyser et al. (2021) found that employees emphasized the need for positivity, as they were "looking for the silver lining" in a situation often considered inherently negative.

Human Factors

Human factors, such as acceptance of and readiness for change at the individual level can make the implementation of change extremely difficult. There is a link between successful organizational change and the perspectives of employees on the effectiveness and desirability of management actions. Neglecting employee perspective can lead to unintended consequences. Cinite et al. (2009) observed that an organization is not considered ready for change by the employees in cases where the employees are not provided with a vision for change, the reasons behind the change, or the expected outcomes and benefits of the transformational change.

Resistance to change can be caused by the fear or uncertainty leading to potential job losses. Competence and commitment of the change agents and the level of participation in the change process by the employees can determine the success or failure of the transformational change.

Readiness for change is an individual-level phenomenon; at an earlier stage of change implementation, positive attitudes toward change are fostered by organizationwide communication, whereas, at a later stage, these attitudes are drawn out with an individual-level approach (Kuntz and Gomes 2012). For an organizational change to succeed, individuals need a proper vision and ideas about outcomes, and have to learn and develop new behaviors to comply with change requirements.

Successful implementation of change is one of the most challenging activities as ~70 percent of change programs resulted in failure, according to some scholars (Cinite et al. 2009; Jansson 2013; Kuntz and Gomes 2012). The failure rate of merged firms in creating value and meeting their desired financial or strategic objectives is a challenge as well. Nguyen and Kleiner (2003) define merger failure as: lowered productivity, labor unrest, higher absenteeism, loss of shareholder value, and in some cases, the dissolution of the partnership. According to William (2005), statistics show that ~50 percent of all mergers and acquisitions fail to achieve the intended results.

The potential causes of merger failure include: agency problems, optimism, and a conflict of interest between the employees in the two merged firms.

Discontent with the communication regarding the organizational changes due to mergers and acquisitions correlates to reluctance, questioning, and low trust in management (Thorwid and Vinge 2020). As change touches on issues close to the hearts of those affected, they will most likely react emotionally due to anxiety or fear of the unknown (Issah 2018) and the ability to handle emotions in mergers and acquisitions may vary depending on the context, according to Sarala et al. (2019). Emotionally intelligent individuals can empathize with others (Miao et al. 2018); however, emotional intelligence has to be specific to the organizational needs to accomplish its goals (Alhamami et al. 2020). Getting employees to commit and be involved in the merger and acquisition process will amplify their feelings of ownership, which, in turn, will lead to the acquired firm retaining their employees postmerger (Degbey et al. 2020) but this requires transformational leadership (Alhamami et al. 2020).

Transformational leaders stimulate thought by soliciting input of others, encouraging followers to challenge old ways of operation, view problems from a new perspective, participate in developing new, more efficient work processes, and overcome resistance to change (McClellan et al. 2017). Emotional intelligence and transformational leadership become more prevalent in a conflict-stricken environment (Alhamami et al. 2020).

Inspirational motivation involves creating a vision that is appealing to others. Leaders with this skill communicate a sense of optimism about the future that is internalized by followers (McClellan et al. 2017). Expressions of emotions vary across cultural settings and thereby reduce the emotional capability of foreign firm employees to interpret emotions correctly (Sarala et al. 2019). However, capturing a firm's culture is not straightforward (Renneboog and Vansteenkiste 2019). According to Issah (2018), the leaders cannot expect others to change if they themselves are not willing to change.

Transformational Change Models

Transformational change requires learning, development, and reflection on the individual's part to understand the desirability, acceptability, and readiness for change. There is a substantial body of literature covering transformational change models, such as Lewin's (1951) three-step change model, Beckhard's (1969) change program, Kotter's (1996) eight-step model for transformational change, and Latta's (2009) OC³ model of organizational change. Similarities and differences between these change models are presented in Table 3.1. The recent models have included additional steps to reflect changing organizational structures and to incorporate organizational culture, even though the concepts introduced by Lewin (1951): unfreezing the current situation, changing and refreezing the new status quo seem to form basis of these models.

The critics of the transformational change models argue that these models are based on the assumption that organizations operate under stable conditions and can move from one stable state to another in a planned manner. Therefore, transformational change models might not be useful in turbulent business environments.

In his critical analysis, D'Ortenzio (2012) asserted that Lewin's model ignores the role of power and politics, and appears too simplistic and mechanistic. For Kotter's model to be successful, all of the eight stages

Table 3.1 Similarities and differences between change models

Lewin (1951) 3-Step model	Beckhard (1969) Change program	Kotter (1996) 8-Step change model	Latta (2009) OC³ model of organizational change
Unfreezing	Analyzing present condition	Sense of urgency Create guiding coalition	Cultural analysis of readiness Shaping vision
Changing	Setting goals for future Plan of action	Develop vision and strategy Communicate the vision Empower employees Generate short-term wins	Informing change initiatives Reflecting culture in implementation Embodying cultural intent Cultural mediation of implementation
Refreezing	Implementing the plan	Improve on the changes Institutionalize new approaches	Moderating outcomes of change Documenting collateral effects

must be worked through in order, skipping even a single step could be problematic, and the model could be seen as a checklist rather than a process, as intended by Kotter.

Anderson and Anderson (2011) in their change process model for leading conscious transformation, suggest that all organizational change requires attention to three central areas: content, people, and process. They argue that being responsive to change is not enough and the companies and their employees must be proactive and prepare for future changes. The content of change is "what" is going to change, including structure, systems, and products. "People" refer to the human side of change, while "process" refers to how the content and people changes will be planned and implemented (Anderson and Anderson 2011).

The first phase of Anderson and Anderson's (2011) model is initiated with the assumption that a consensus exists in the organization that there is a need for change. D'Ortenzio (2012) warns that employees might not accept change, if they see no reason for it. Even if the need for change is identified and agreed upon, it is almost impossible to have a homogeneous approach to the process, pace, and practical implications of change. The model does not include any form of external intervention. The learning comes from breakthroughs, cross-training, and shared best practices from within the organization. Emotional aspects of change such as anxiety, stress, and fear appear to have been overlooked in the rather simplistic assumption of cross-training and shared best practices during a transformational change. The evidence base of Anderson and Anderson's (2011) model is limited to their own observations and experiences and the model does not seem to take into consideration vital human factors, for instance distrust, apathy, fear, and anxiety. The change models presented in Table 3.1, particularly the latter ones, show more appreciation for human and cultural factors.

Transformational change models do not seem to take into consideration the transformative learning of staff during the process of change in the organizational context. The focal point of these transformational change models appears to be the management of staff rather than the development of staff. Additionally, these models are directed at organizations in need of change but otherwise operating in a stable environment, which is not the case with many organizations.

Coaching and Mentoring

Coaching and mentoring are developmental interventions but the literature shows that there are different, sometimes contradictory descriptions of these fields. Therefore, we start by discussing how coaching and mentoring are perceived by different scholars and practitioners from within the coaching and mentoring fields in order to explore the existing literature and to highlight the contradictions. Several theories including career development theory, social network theory, human capital theory, and adult learning theory from related disciplines—such as economics, psychology, philosophy, leadership, and management—that underpin coaching and mentoring fields are relevant. Confusion about coaching and mentoring terminology is highlighted by many scholars and practitioners, and some of them suggest that a lack of clear distinction benefits related disciplines such as counseling and training. It is not clear from the literature how coaches and mentors (or providers of these services) perceive and distinguish between the coaching and mentoring fields. The impact of human factors such as fear, stress, and anxiety on the success or failure of organizational changes is also discussed.

Theoretical Base of Coaching and Mentoring Fields

In this section, we discuss the theoretical debate about coaching and mentoring. There are various definitions and criteria used by different authors and practitioners to describe and distinguish coaching and mentoring. Some practitioners seem to be unclear about the distinction between coaching and mentoring, and use the terms loosely. This lack of clarity has to be highlighted for two reasons: (1) a clear distinction is vital for coaching and mentoring to become established and theoretically informed fields and (2) clarity from the respondents' perspective is important for a better understanding of the impact of coaching or mentoring on implementing transformational change.

Coaching and mentoring are classed as different fields based on theory and practice. Grant and Cavanagh (2004) claim that coaching is theoretically grounded and systematic, while Hezlett and Gibson (2005) argue that mentoring research, theory, and practice has a solid foundation.

Rogers (2012, 1) asserts that "the terminology of mentoring and coaching in the literature has been confused or remains confusing." Kram and Isabella (1985) include coaching as one of the mentoring interventions. They argue that mentoring provides career-enhancing functions, such as sponsorship, coaching, and facilitating exposure and visibility to help young people establish a role, learn the ropes, and prepare for advancement. Meanwhile, Lord et al. (2008, 12) acknowledge conceptual differences between coaching and mentoring, but argue that the "overall ingredients of mentoring and coaching are reasonably similar." However, while Bresser and Wilson (2010) agree about the similarities, they highlight "fundamental differences" between the roles of a coach and a mentor. They assert that a mentor has experience in a particular field and imparts specific knowledge, acting as advisor, counselor, guide, tutor, or teacher. In contrast, the coach's role is not to advise but to assist coachees in uncovering their own knowledge and skills and to facilitate coachees in becoming their own advisors. Rogers (2012) observed a coaching and mentoring role reversal. She claims:

> Academics have tended to position coaching as an activity which aims at performance only, meaning a minor adjustment to behaviour, whereas they have linked mentoring to a transformational learning outcome, where the learner experiences a total change in how they view the world. However, the recent expansion of coaching as a developmental method insists that coaching aims at transformation as a learning outcome, and mentors are simply company advisors or even inexpensive tutors (Rogers 2012, 1).

It appears that in Roger's observation, ultimately the term "mentoring" has been diluted from a transformational activity to cheap tutoring, whereas "coaching" has established itself from one of the mentoring interventions to a developmental method for transformation and learning. Regardless of this shift in perception, both coaching and mentoring seem to have become popular developmental interventions. Because of their increasing popularity, other professions related to coaching and mentoring, such as counseling, training, and human resources development, are "trying to stake out the territory with definitions, rules, and practices based on its own particular perspectives and interests" (Clutterbuck 2008, 8). Kram and Isabella (1985) found common attributes between mentoring and peer relationships. They assert that in a hierarchical organization the individual is likely to have more peers than bosses or mentors. Kram and Isabella (1985, 128) identified peer relationships to be in the categories of "information peer, collegial peer, and special peer." They argue that both mentoring and peer relationships have the potential to support development at successive career stages, and both provide a range of career-enhancing and psychological functions. Garvey (2004, 6) asserts that counseling, in addition to coaching and mentoring, assists people to learn and develop; he refers to the phenomenon as "helping." Coaching and mentoring "appear in different guises" according to Lord et al. (2008, 9), while Hamlin et al. (2008), in their comparative study, concluded that human resource development and coaching are virtually the same. The aforementioned shows that there may be a vested interest in keeping the definitions inconclusive and boundaries blurred in an attempt to cash in on the success of coaching and mentoring.

Coaching and mentoring do not seem to have established a theoretical base yet. This paucity of coaching and mentoring theories has been acknowledged by various authors. The absence of a theoretical base in coaching is related to the lack of critical evaluation of commercially sensitive coaching models, which are "rigorously guarded," according to Cavanagh and Grant (2005, vi). They state:

> ...good theories [of coaching] are frustratingly hard to come by ... [and] creating good theory is a dialectical process. It involves repeated processes of construction and testing followed by more construction and more testing ... [T]here is a multitude of relatively untested proprietary coaching models in the market place ... which are ultimately supported by little more than anecdotal evidence, personal conviction and blind optimism (Cavanagh and Grant 2005, vi, vii).

Although lacking a theoretical base of their own, the coaching and mentoring fields have been informed by a broad base of related disciplines with an established theoretical grounding: for instance, adult learning (Cox 2006), psychodynamics and organizational theory (Orenstein 2007), psychology, and psychotherapy (Rogers 2012). Grant (2005) suggests that coaching practices are underpinned by four key knowledge domains: the behavioral sciences, business and economic science, adult education (including workplace learning and development), and philosophy.

In contrast, mentoring has benefited from other areas. In their analysis, Ehrich et al. (2001) found that mentoring is underpinned by a range of theoretical perspectives. They put these theoretical perspectives into nine categories: economics, developmental theories, the authors' own theory, the selection process of mentoring, theories related to power, leadership/management theory, learning theory, theories related to organizational structure/socialization, and networks and theories related to interpersonal relationships (Ehrich et al. 2001). Learning and development in these theories involves a change in an individual's knowledge, and in his or her ability to perform a skill or participate in an activity with other individuals. There are variations among these theories about the nature of change, as a result of learning and development. However, transformative change through reflection seems to be the bedrock of adult learning theories, as identified by Mezirow (1991). Reflection is a central process of transformative learning, which "may result in transformation" (Mezirow 1991, 6). The self-reflection supported by coaching and mentoring can result in "heightened self-awareness, self-acceptance, increased self-discovery, self-confidence, self-expression, better communication, and problem-solving skills" (Griffiths 2005, 57).

The ability to think critically, reflect on ones' own assumptions and to change the frame of reference is important for personal learning and growth. Personal transformation usually begins with a disorientating dilemma, and the process includes critical reflection, self-examination, and a reorientation that results in revised action and deep learning. The theory of adult transformational learning is grounded in the concept of individual and personal learning and growth, according to Gloss (2013), and it focuses on changes in the perspectives of individuals (Henderson 2002). The terms "transformative learning" and "transformational learning" are used interchangeably in the literature. Transformative learning can only occur when individuals have the capacity to be critically self-reflective and to exercise reflective judgment. Self-reflection promotes awareness, clarifies thinking, generates insights, facilitates new learning, and promotes individual development (Zachary 2005). Coaching and mentoring are utilized to enhance reflection.

To summarize this section, coaching and mentoring can mean different things to different people in different fields and practices, based on their own understanding and interpretation. It is not the aim of this book to settle the coaching and mentoring debate, but to report the role of coaching and mentoring within mergers and transformational change situations. However, by noting how coaching and mentoring are perceived by different scholars and practitioners from varied milieu, the diversity of these fields is emphasized. In the absence of an established theoretical base, coaching and mentoring studies have benefited from a range of related disciplines, including adult transformational learning, career development, psychology, psychodynamics, philosophy, leadership, and management. Workplace theories relating to social learning, personal and professional development, social capital and organizational change also play a role in the theoretical underpinning of coaching and mentoring.

Effectiveness of Coaching

The effectiveness of coaching is an ongoing theme of debate in the field of personal and workplace coaching. Wales (2003) asserts that coaching at work would lead to enhanced confidence, enabling the coachee to deal effectively with issues both at work and at home.

There is an argument that coaching is linked to performance management in which poorly performing employees are offered coaching to improve their organizational performance. Because deeply held beliefs and behaviors can inhibit performance and coaching is used in some organizations as a remedy for poor performance. Grant and Cavanagh (2004) argue that performance coaching deals with the processes by which the coachee can set goals, overcome obstacles, and evaluate and monitor his or her own performance. In their study, Robinson-Walker (2012) noted that most health care and nurse leaders in the United States still viewed coaching as a code for an intervention for poor performance.

In contrast, performance appraisal, where an employee's performance is usually evaluated once a year, has been replaced by performance management, where performance is evaluated on an ongoing basis. Therefore, coaching forms part of performance management in terms of setting and aligning goals and developing employees.

Effectiveness of Mentoring

Mentoring is a developing phenomenon and mentoring arrangements can be found in various settings. A growing body of academic and practitioner literature supports the popular perception that mentoring offers considerable value to individuals and organizations. Hezlett and Gibson (2005) conducted a thorough review of past theories, research, and practices on mentoring through the lens of human resources development, and noted that recent research and theory-building efforts highlight the potential importance of the role of learning in mentoring relationships. They assert that it is important for human resources departments to integrate mentoring with other organizational initiatives to ensure the strategic alignment of programs and practices. Even though mentoring is used in various settings, the focus of this book is specific to mentoring in mergers and transformational change within the workplace context, other mentoring studies, such as youth mentoring and student–faculty mentoring are not explored in this chapter.

Mentoring is "more readily available as an antidote to stress than previously considered" (Kram and Hall 1989, 493) and mentoring relationships are perceived as more desirable during times of workplace stress, resulting from corporate downsizing. Siegel (2000) asserts that during mergers and other changes, organizations use fewer resources "while expecting employees to assume more responsibilities and wider ranges of tasks."

Traditional mentoring relationships involve a mentor and a protégé who are bound together by close ties, engaging in an exchange that involves both career-related and psychosocial resources (Baugh and Fagenson-Eland 2005). Mentoring offered from within the organization which we can refer to as internal mentoring is generally to support the protégés in settling in the new role or preparing for a new role.

However, external mentoring, where the mentor is external to the organization, can lead to more independence and greater career self-efficacy, which is important in changing organizational circumstances such as mergers.

Dymock (1999) found that in a structured mentoring program, mentors benefit from improved self-organization and networking opportunities. He conducted a case study of a major Australian company, which utilizes mentoring as part of its leadership training for potential supervisors. The course was in-house, part-time, over 10 months. The benefits of this program for mentees included: a broader understanding of the company's policies and place in the business world, an appreciation of how management principles might apply in practice, increased knowledge specific to their work areas, and less tangible benefits such as improved self-organization, and opportunities for networking. In their empirical study, Thurston et al. (2012) note that mentoring programs offer leaders hope for influencing the characteristics of individual employees in a way that can be beneficial to both the employee and the organization. They found that mentoring had a direct and statistically significant impact on employees' contribution to their organization's success.

Mentoring relationships provide a context for the transfer of learning, but conventional mentoring is also a way of reinforcing organizational traditions, politics, and culturally appropriate behavior:

Conventional mentoring seeks sameness in terms of both fidelity with and reproduction of extant organisational culture. The purpose of [the] relationship is for development along stipulated paths for the achievement of stipulated outcomes. The learning outcomes here can only be those of adaptation, error prevention or correction, or reduction of deviation: single loop processes (Bokeno and Gantt 2000, 249).

Traditional mentoring relationships no longer work, according to Kram and Higgins (2012). They proposed a network model of mentoring, which involves a group (as opposed to a one-to-one) relationship, the mentor and the mentee are colearners (unlike mentors guiding mentees) and the mentoring relationship extends beyond the organizational boundary (it is both inside and outside the organization). The network model of mentoring is expected to yield overlap in enhanced performance and leadership capacity at both individual and organizational levels. Additionally, the individual outcomes can include learning, self-awareness, and social skills, while the organization can benefit from retention, organizational learning, and innovation.

Workplace Learning

There is a small but growing body of knowledge that examines the effect of workplace coaching on stress. Describing the impact of organizational change, restructuring, and mergers on employees, Grant (2013, 5) noted:

> *Organisational changes typically create stress for employees and managers as they re-calibrate their working practices in response to a shifting and turbulent corporate landscape whilst simultaneously striving to achieve their designated organisational goal.*

Coaching helps increase self-confidence and personal insight, which helps participants to deal with organizational change. In their randomized-controlled study of Australian public health workers, Grant et al. (2009) found that coaching enhances goal attainment, increases resilience and workplace well-being, and reduces depression and stress. In their study of the UK finance sector and the Scandinavian telecommunications sector, Gyllensten and Palmer (2006) found that coaching indirectly helps to reduce workplace stress. They reported that coaching helps participants by reducing role ambiguity, improving confidence, and enhancing assertiveness. All these factors indirectly reduce workplace stress. Therefore, the organizations that are planning major changes might benefit from coaching to help employees through the period of change. Coaching significantly increases the participants' goal attainment, solution-focused thinking, and readiness for change.

Conclusion

The focus of this book is on the role of coaching and mentoring during transformational changes, with specific emphasis on change resulting from mergers and acquisitions. Confusion about coaching and mentoring terminology is highlighted by many scholars and practitioners, and some of them suggest that a lack of clear distinction benefits related disciplines such as counseling and training. It is not clear from the literature how coaches and mentors (or providers of these services) perceive and distinguish between the coaching and mentoring fields. The extent to which perceptions about coaching and mentoring influence the choice of potential coachees about their development is not clear either. With reference to the negative connotations attached to coaching (for instance, as a remedy for poor performance), we believe that understanding the perceptions of potential coachees will serve a useful purpose. By addressing these gaps, this study can inform theory and practice in these areas.

Organizational change is known for the negative consequences it has for employees, including uncertainty, fear, and stress. Coaching enhances personal insight and self-confidence, which may enable staff to deal effectively with stress. Mentoring strengthens the relationship between the mentor and the protégé. Coaching and mentoring interventions provide psychological support to cope with the stress and anxiety created by the merger or transformational change.

However, the empirical evidence from quantitative studies conducted thus far regarding the effectiveness of coaching to overcome stress and anxiety is inconclusive. The case for using coaching and mentoring to address the effects of transformational change and mergers is as yet unproven.

Transformational change models applicable in the workplace context focus on the management rather than the development of staff. Besides, transformational change concentrates on changing the whole organization while transformational learning invokes reflection to change the perspective of individuals. Although there are some transformational change models that do include coaching and mentoring for learning and development, these are set in the education sector (regarding the learning and development of students); hence there is a lack of focus on the workplace context.

Jansson (2013, 1003), in her critical analysis, challenged the taken-for-granted "mundane assumptions" in the organizational change literature. She argues that certain elements (such as universal patterns and assumptions about resistance to change) particular to one organization should not be universally applied to all organizational change situations. Readiness for change is an individual-level phenomenon; at an earlier stage of change implementation, positive attitudes toward change are fostered by organizationwide communication, whereas, at a later stage, these attitudes are drawn out with an individual-level approach (Kuntz and Gomes, 2012). For an organizational change to succeed, individuals need a proper vision and ideas about outcomes, and have to learn and develop new behaviors to comply with change requirements.

Human factors, such as acceptance of and readiness for change at the individual level, conflict of interest, and cultural incompatibility are the key attributes of the success or failure of a merger or transformational change, according to the aforementioned studies. Kiefer (2002) argues that emotions help individuals to adapt to difficult situations and drive behaviors, and they constitute the construction of the individual and social meaning of the change process. Anxiety that might have an impact on the success or failure of mergers is likely to be caused by the uncertainty and anticipated negative impact on the individual's career. Marks and Mirvis (1997) warn that a lack of communication from senior executives will amplify stress and anxiety.

In sum, transformational change and mergers give rise to anxiety, perceived uncertainty, and stress. These human factors play a role in the success or failure of a transformational change or merger. In the next chapter, studies discussing the use of mentoring to deal with human factors in organizational change contexts are evaluated.

CHAPTER 4

Mentoring

Introduction

The mentoring programs used by various organizations are presented in this chapter. Before evaluating the effectiveness of mentoring in the transformational change context, we will discuss some mentoring arrangements. Most organizations have their own organization-specific mentoring programs, such as McDonalds' "Where You Want To Be;" however, the focus of this chapter is to explore wide ranging, cross-sectional, and cross-organizational mentoring programs and how such programs can help implement organizational change. The mentoring relationships discussed here are as follows: (1) industry-specific mentoring, (2) executive mentoring, (3) peer mentoring, and (4) empowerment mentoring.

In the industry-specific mentoring program, middle to senior managers from under-represented groups within an organization are mentored by senior executives from another organization within the same industry or sector. For example, an engineering firm with fewer female managers might enter into mentoring arrangement with another engineering firm that champions gender balance. Learning and development of both the mentor and the mentee is enhanced by sharing knowledge and reflecting on the effectiveness of different tools and techniques used during the mentoring process. Such programs do not generally cater for the developmental needs of senior executives responsible for initiating and managing change, even though it develops middle to senior managers who have responsibility for implementing change in their departments.

In executive mentoring, senior officials receive mentoring from external coaches. These coaches share their knowledge and experience, which is accumulated from the public and private sectors. This type of mentoring relationship provides an out-of-sector perspective for the executives, which can be helpful while evaluating strategic options.

Peer mentoring can focus on streamlining the front-line services following the merger. In this mentoring arrangement, best practices at operational level are shared with staff from the recently merged organizations.

The mentoring arrangements mentioned so far, are aimed at the development of staff. Induction, peer, and out-of-sector mentoring do contribute to the effective and efficient management of mergers. However, in some cases, organizations train and mentor people, who are not their employees. The aim of this empowerment mentoring could be to help unemployed people into employment by providing a mentor, a safe space to learn a trade, and to improve their employability.

Industry-Specific Mentoring Program

Here, I use an example of Housing Diversity Network (HDN) mentoring program that was used in England to develop the leadership skills of managers working in the social housing sector. The housing associations, own and manage a large number of houses sometimes over 100,000 and these houses are rented out to the tenants who can't afford or choose not to buy their own houses. The HDN started providing mentoring within housing associations in 2005. At that time, mergers between housing associations were entering into a phase where different housing groups had started merging to form bigger housing groups. However, the HDN mentoring programs did not initially focus on housing association mergers or transformational change. The mentoring was to address the under-representation of Black Minority Ethnic (BME) groups in housing association management. There is no shift in the focus of the mentoring program to incorporate mergers or transformational changes.

HDN mentoring is a classic example of industry-specific mentoring program. The network provides dedicated support, which includes initial training, templates for how to structure mentoring sessions, ongoing support for the mentors and the mentees during the mentorship period, and award ceremonies to recognize the successful completion of the mentoring programs.

Potential mentors, who are senior housing executives are required to have skills and experience in a particular area before applying to become mentors. A database of potential mentors and mentees is maintained.

By introducing mentors with certain specialities to their potential mentees, who aspire to develop those specialities, the HDN plays the role of a matchmaker. But sometimes the specific requirements of the mentees cannot be matched from within the pool of existing mentors. In these cases, the potential mentors are contacted through their professional networks, that is. Chartered Institute of housing, and invited to offer mentoring services.

Testimonials on the HDN website describe the benefits of the mentoring arrangement, which include gaining: an independent sounding board, objective feedback, personal development, reinforced knowledge, the building of confidence, and a broadening of housing knowledge. These are presumed to be transferable skills for both the mentor and the mentee and both parties can benefit from the mentoring program in terms of their own personal development. The mentors share their wisdom, tools, and techniques with the mentees; subsequently, they receive feedback from the mentees about the usefulness of these tools and techniques in different organizational settings. Learning taken from the evaluation and reflection is incorporated in the next round of mentoring.

Reflection on the effectiveness of different tools and techniques not only enhances the mentee's learning but also inspires mentors to reflect on their own practice.

Another form of industry-specific mentoring program can be the provision of internal mentoring within larger organizations. In these cases, as part of the professional development of managers (potential mentees), an executive is allocated as a mentor, with the mentee's agreement. Usually, the mentor would be an executive from another company within the same group, or an executive from a different department of the same company, but never the line manager of the mentee.

In the industry-specific mentoring program, the appointment of mentors varies depending upon the developmental aspirations of the potential mentor and the expertise sought by the potential mentee. The mentees are described as "leaders of tomorrow." The request to seek mentoring is approved because these managers are viewed as having high potential for promotion.

The industry-specific mentoring program seems to support experimentation and learning from the success and failure of different tools and techniques. McKimm et al. (2007, 5) note that learning and experimentation in a mentoring relationship occurs through "analysis, examination, re-examination, and reflection on practice, situations, problems, mistakes, and successes of both the mentor and the mentee." Mentoring provides continued professional development and mutual growth for both the mentor and the mentee, as suggested by a number of authors, such as Oliver and Aggleton (2002), Hezlett and Gibson (2005), and Ragins and Kram (2007). Even though, the mentor holds the experience, knowledge, and skills that the mentee needs, desires, and aspires to master; the mentoring relationship develops congruently, as described by Jacobson et al. (2012), and both the mentor and the mentee seem to benefit from this learning experience.

One of the significant features of the industry-specific mentoring program is that the mentor and the mentee are both from the same industry but from different organizations. Such an arrangement seems ideal to help mentees in dealing with workplace problems they may not want to share with their own managers (Dymock 1999). In spite of this, Hatmaker et al. (2011) argue that organizational and task-based knowledge is tacit, grounded in the experience of more senior co-workers, supervisors, and upper-level managers, and ties should be developed to access this information. This is not always the case, as the mentor and the mentee are rarely co-workers in the industry-specific leadership development mentoring programs. However, Baugh and Fagenson-Eland (2005) argue that nothing in the definition of mentoring suggests that the mentor and the mentee must be employed in the same organization.

The industry-specific mentoring program can be classed as contract mentoring. Patel et al. (2011, 419) describe contract mentoring as "formal mentoring that was created for a specific purpose within a set time-frame." Additionally, this mentoring program appears to have elements of competency mentoring. In competency mentoring, according to Patel et al. (2011, 419), "the mentor demonstrates and aids the mentee to achieve a set of competencies." Demonstrating how to perform surgery to a trainee surgeon (mentee) could be a crucial part of mentoring, as Patel et al.'s (2011) study was about the mentorship of newly qualified surgeons, but it is not appropriate in all industry-specific mentoring arrangements.

Clutterbuck, in his blog (April 12, 2012) describes cross-organizational mentoring in which a small number of mentoring programs are facilitated by a consortium of organizations for their employees. He asserts that some public sector organizations such as local authorities, health trusts, police, and fire services have formed consortia to share resources.

In summation, the industry-specific mentoring programs are focused on developing future leaders. Senior executives act as mentors, not mentees. The industry-specific mentoring program does not have a mechanism in place to facilitate the mentoring of senior executives. Many organizations are significantly changing and are increasingly becoming large and complex organizations. Senior executives who are leading these organizations through a merger or transformational change can benefit from being mentored through this process. The mentoring program develops managers to implement change in their departments but it does not help senior executives to initiate and manage organizational change.

This gap is being filled by external coaches, who act as mentors to senior housing executives. This arrangement is discussed in the next section.

External Coaches Acting As Mentors

Some senior executives receive mentoring from external coaches, under themes such as, "the development and growth of senior managers." However, the mentoring agenda, according to the coaches, is not about the personal or professional development of these senior executives in readiness for the next promotion, but about dealing with the challenges at hand. The underlying purpose of mentoring varies from identifying strategic direction, learning from the private sector, or gaining an external perspective. This section reflects the experiences and observations of external coaches who act as mentors for senior executives dealing with a merger or an acquisition or other transformational change.

It comes across from one of the coach's accounts that some senior executives are struggling to find a strategic direction in the wake of organizational challenges.

There is a bit about, in these challenging times, how do you help senior management actually have a vision within an organisation?

The external coaches, who are the mentors in this arrangement, have broader experience, which includes working in and providing mentoring for different sectors, including the for-profit sector and entrepreneurship. This experience appeals to the senior executives in choosing their mentors.

Some senior executives working in not-for-profit sector look to the private sector with a view to understand how organizational change is managed as a result of a merger or restructure. This out-of-sector perspective enables these executives to address some of their own issues effectively. Motive behind the choice of mentor can be: the quest for innovation and entrepreneurship, nurturing skills of the mentors, and their objectivity.

Newly appointed or promoted senior executives can benefit from the nurturing skills of the mentors by developing ideas for revenue generation. At the same time, experienced executives wishing to launch new initiatives will find the nurturing skills and objectivity of the mentors useful. External coaches provide not only a safe environment to explore fresh ideas but also an objective viewpoint about the workability and feasibility of any such ideas. Furthermore, they can help the senior executives in nurturing those ideas.

Change is the order of the day for many organizations, but there is little evidence of peer mentoring at the executive level to deal with organizational change. Additionally, industry-specific mentoring programs discussed earlier do not include merger or transformational change-related mentoring for senior executives. The managers who do receive industry-specific mentoring are not in a position to initiate organizationwide change through their personal and professional development as a direct result of the mentoring. This is because they hold operational rather than strategic positions in the organizational hierarchy. Therefore, they are only responsible for implementing changes in their own departments.

Cases of executives seeking mentoring from external coaches for their nurturing and entrepreneurial skills, can be interpreted in a number of ways: (1) the executives could be considering incorporating some of the practices adopted by the private sector, (2) it could be seen as a skills deficit in the areas of entrepreneurship and change management among the current mentors within certain industry sector, or (3) it could possibly be due to the commercial sensitivity and confidentiality necessitated by the complex organizational change within an organization.

The scope of this out-of-sector mentoring is more wide-ranging than traditional mentor–protégé relationships. This type of mentoring provides additional confidentiality for commercially sensitive issues, and provides the mentees with an opportunity to benefit from the mentors' experience in exploring innovative entrepreneurial initiatives.

Executive mentoring discussed in this section is an example of out-of-sector mentoring, which is not uncommon according to Jacobson et al. (2012), because such an arrangement would benefit senior executives looking for innovative ideas to manage change. The challenge for public sector leaders is to be brave, competent, and passionate if they want to foster innovation and entrepreneurship (Bóo 2008). Mentoring can help in managing and coping with the pace of change (Garvey 2004; Bamford 2011).

To take up the challenge of being innovative and brave, as noted by Bóo (2008), the executives have to explore and identify opportunities to save costs and generate additional income in their organizations. The mentoring relationship needs to be based on openness and trust (Dymock 1999), which might be hard to achieve if both the mentor and mentee were senior executives in different organizations within the same sector, because of commercial sensitivity.

Peer Mentoring As Part of Postmerger Staff Induction

Peer mentoring is sometimes referred to as: job shadowing, buddy system, and peer mentoring. In some cases, organizations use induction mentoring as part of the postmerger staff induction programs. As all mergers result in some sort of restructure, one of the aims of this induction mentoring can be to familiarize staff with the new organizational structure. This postmerger induction is significantly different from induction offered to newly recruited employees or other mentoring programs for staff development, such as McDonalds' "Where You Want To Be."

The postmerger induction mentoring helps staff in understanding the roles and responsibilities of their colleagues working in different departments. The organizations can use this opportunity to make staff aware of the culture, vision, and strategic objectives of the newly merged group.

We have a structured induction programme, where staff from the merged organisations come in, they meet their colleagues, have a number of different presentations about the key parts of the organisation, meet various teams, spend a little bit of time with each of the teams just to see what they all do, to get to know people.

The structured nature of the induction mentoring highlights the importance of teamwork in newly merged organizations. Understanding the roles and responsibilities of different teams through presentations and then meeting and spending time with colleagues from different teams should enhance team cohesion.

Human factors such as stress and anxiety arising from uncertainty and concerns about job security during the course of a merger are allayed during the induction mentoring. The friendly welcome and a structured program gives the impression that the hectic change period is coming to an end, and can ultimately result in reduced fear and insecurity. The programs also provide positive vibes in the form of the strategic direction of the organization.

In addition to the induction mentoring, some organization offers peer mentoring for the new staff after the merger or restructure. This peer mentoring is comparatively less formal, longer term, and only available to the nonmanagerial staff. The arrangement can be referred to as the "buddy system" or "job shadowing." The time spent with the mentors in this buddy system is aimed at helping them learn the ropes. The buddy system focuses on operational aspects and the "working processes" of the job. Finding out about the roles and responsibilities of new colleagues after the merger can enhance team collaboration.

Two modes of peer mentoring, following the merger can emerge. In the case of an organization joining a larger group, the processes and procedures of the group prevail. Officials working in the group peer–mentor their colleagues from the newly merged organization. In the case of a "merger of equals," where two organizations merged to form a bigger group, the better-quality procedures are adopted. It is not uncommon to find inconsistencies in the quality of the processes and procedures among different organizations prior to the merger.

One part of the organisation can be much more forward in terms of its processes, and its procedures are much more in line with the industry regulators' requirements, whereas the other organisation can be somewhat less concerned about the constitution and the regulation. In these cases, after the merger, the systems of the most compliant organisation has to be implemented in the less compliant organisation.

Implementing the "better-quality" procedures of one organization in all the other organizations within the group after the merger or acquisition can cause some disquiet and resistance. This can lead to the affected staff starting to say things like, *we are being taken over … we are being told what to do.* This indicates that peer mentoring in the merger of equals might be more challenging than in a case where a small organization is taken over by a larger group. This distinction is important, because of the potential staffing issues such as tension and conflict during peer mentoring following the merger.

Induction mentoring serves an important purpose in effective integration, according to some authors such as Garvey (2004), Dymock (1999), and Thurston et al. (2012). Describing the induction process, Fox et al. (2005) conclude that induction for new staff members includes the provision of adequate guidance and assistance through buddying with a preceptor. In line with the findings of Dymock (1999), induction mentoring appears to provide mentees with a broader understanding of the organizations' policies and corporate vision. In an empirical study, Thurston et al. (2012) noted that mentoring programs offered leaders a way to influence the characteristics of individual employees in a way that can be beneficial to both the employee and the organization.

Patel et al. (2011, 419) describe the induction program for trainee surgeons as an example of pseudo-mentoring: mentoring in "appearance only," which focused on specific tasks for a short period of time. It can be true in the case of newly merged organizations that offer induction mentoring for a couple of weeks, but it is not in appearance only. This is aimed at helping merged staff to settle into the new role, in the case of an organization being taken over by a larger group, or to adopt to a changed role if the policies and procedures have changed.

Peer mentoring has been discussed by some authors, like Siegel (2000), Fox et al. (2005), and Patel et al. (2011) in the context of newly appointed staff. Kram and Isabella (1985), Siegel (2000), and Hatmaker et al. (2011) found the formal or informal peer relationship useful, whereas Patel et al. (2011) described peer mentoring as pseudo-mentoring in their model. However, according to Hatmaker et al. (2011) job shadowing or peer mentoring is helpful in understanding and adapting to the new ways of working following the merger. It can enhance enculturation and embeddedness within the organization. The peer mentoring can have an element of "competency mentoring" (Patel et al. 2011), as the mentors demonstrate to their colleagues how they are doing their job. Mentoring in newly merged organizations can help in dealing with organizational change-related uncertainty, stress, and anxiety.

In conclusion, peer mentoring is not only relevant for newly appointed staff, but some organizations use it after the merger as well. Second, in a merger situation, peer mentoring can be seen by the participants negatively or positively, depending on the relative position of their employer. In the case of a small organization being taken over by a large group, peer mentoring can be valued by staff, but in a merger of equals, the employees receiving peer mentoring to learn new procedures after the merger might show antipathy toward it. This element of apprehension among peers in the merger of equals and its adverse impact on the postmerger peer mentoring relationships should not be overlooked.

Empowerment Mentoring

Mentoring can empower under-represented groups, enhance gender balance in organizations, generate efficiencies within the supply chain, and facilitate employability in the communities that are served by the organizations. Offering mentoring service for the activities listed above or other empowering initiatives is a worthwhile cause. The organizations benefit from: positive business reputation, brand recognition, increased customer loyalty, and in some cases easier access to capital. Empowerment mentoring can help the society in better employment opportunities, economic development, technology and infrastructure, and higher standard of living.

The cross-organizational mentoring arrangement is generally developed by leading organizations from different industries or sectors with a mission to address the scarcity of leadership positions held by important but under-represented groups in the society. For example, developing mentoring arrangements for women in what is commonly said as male-dominated industries or vice a versa.

In some cases, industry-specific mentoring programs are not the right platform to deal with a deeper societal issue, such as gender balance, under-represented or even neglected certain groups, and communities or even the mentoring people to deal with a previously neglected or not foreseen global issue. Because of the nature or severity of the issue, leading organizations join forces to provide a mentoring platform. One example of such platforms is, the Network of Executive Women (NEW). The NEW's mission is "to advance women, grow business. and transform our industry's workplace through the power of community" and their vision is a workplace with no limits. This network focuses on the betterment of women serving in retail, consumer goods, financial services, and technology industries.

Toyota Mentorship Program (TMP) for small and diverse businesses aims to help businesses that may lack the technical expertise or skills to compete more effectively in their given market. This mentorship program has forged partnerships with several organizations, including Women's Business Council Southwest, Women's Business Enterprise Council, and North Texas LGBT (Lesbian, Gay, Bisexual, and Transgender) Chamber of Commerce to identify and upskill new mentees to bridge the skills gap.

Johnson & Johnson offers mentorship from the platform of Fortune/U.S. State Department Global Women's Mentoring Partnership. The goal of this mentoring initiative is to equip international mentees with invaluable knowledge that they can use to bolster their own business back home and inspire positive change in their local communities.

Blackstone Chambers is one of the six Barristers' Chambers in England and Wales working together to create a mentoring scheme for underrepresented groups at the Bar. The under-represented groups for this mentoring scheme include women, people from minority ethnic backgrounds, people with disabilities, LGBT + people, people who spent time in care, and people from different socioeconomic backgrounds. It is open to undergraduates and graduates from under-represented groups noted previously who do not yet have a pupillage offer. The mentoring program includes one-on-one meetings between the mentee and the mentor, workshops on application for pupillage, and social events.

Similar mentoring programs are offered by some Housing Associations in the UK. Initiatives, such as mentoring into employment are used by some organizations to tackle unemployment in the communities they serve.

As part of their transforming neighborhoods initiative, the housing associations mentor tenants into employment. Some of the properties owned and managed by these housing association are situated in the most deprived areas in the UK. There is high unemployment and the neighborhoods are cluttered with antisocial issues, including loan sharks, drugs, and gun-related crimes. In an effort to transform the neighborhoods, the housing associations have already introduced different initiatives to improve the housing estates. These initiatives include police surgeries in local housing offices and joint walkabouts of the estates, in which tenant groups and housing officials go round and meet tenants on their doorsteps. Initiatives like mentoring tenants into employment are fully supported by the board of directors.

In this initiative, tenants in long-term unemployment are offered on-the-job training and mentoring to equip them with employability skills. When the manager responsible for mentoring program feels that these tenants are fully trained, then they are supported with their job application and mentored for the interview process.

Mentoring under-represented or disadvantaged groups into employment offers corporate rewards for the organizations that offer these initiatives, as the mentees become ambassadors of these organizations.

Mentoring under-represented or disadvantaged groups into employment is an example of apprenticeship mentoring. Patel et al. (2011, 419) explained that in apprenticeship mentoring, "the mentee learns by observing and emulating mentor's skills." The mentor demonstrated and aided the mentees in learning and practicing their skills to achieve a set of competencies, which is described by Patel et al. (2011) as competency mentoring. So the empowerment mentoring programs are a combination of apprenticeship mentoring and competency mentoring, according to the classification of Patel et al. (2011).

Mentoring into employment or promotion seems to illustrate Oliver and Aggleton's (2002, 33) contention that the apprenticeship model of mentoring incorporates "watching and emulating experienced profession-als in the workplace". The recognition of mentoring manager's work at high profile award ceremonies can enhance the sense of achievement and motivation of the recipient and have considerable value both for the men-tor (Hezlett and Gibson, 2005) and the organization.

Learning and development through mentoring adds to the work of Oliver and Aggleton (2002) and Lord et al. (2008), who note that mentoring is widely used in the local government and not-for-profit sectors in the UK. Industry-specific mentoring and senior executives' mentoring by external coaches are examples of transformative learning. The double-loop learning (Argyris, 1987) addresses personal assumptions, challenges beliefs (Henderson, 2002), and improves practice through ongoing critical reflection. Conversely, mentoring under-represented groups, peer mentoring, and induction mentoring focus on passing on skills and showing the ropes. According to Argyris and Schön (1978), where the emphasis is on techniques and making techniques more efficient, it is single-loop learning. This leads to development but not the transformation.

The analysis in this chapter has illustrated different mentoring programs used within various organizations. Due to the diverse range of developmental needs of mentees, a single mentorship model is not appro-priate. To accommodate most, if not all, variables would make any such model too complex, and its universal application questionable.

A common feature of the four mentoring programs is that they all enhance the learning and development of both the mentors and the mentees. Cox (1999, ii) classed mentoring as a "burgeoning activity" occurring in various organizational settings. A report by McKimm et al. (2007) discusses the mentoring schemes used in different professional settings, such as medicine, nursing, physiotherapy, occupational ther-apy, and education. This chapter adds the merger and transformational change-related examples of the utilization of mentoring. The complex-ity of interlinking various programs is discussed here. Each program has its unique features, so it is not right to bundle them together. However, by interlinking common features, some meaningful conclusions can be reached to inform mentoring practice, the transformational change and mentoring literature, and transformative learning theory.

Summary

In the industry-specific mentoring and induction and peer mentoring, both the mentor and the mentee are serving officials in the same organization but the nature of the mentoring relationship is different. The industry-specific mentoring provides a platform for managers to learn from the best in the sector. Thus the industry as a whole benefits from the community of competent practitioners. The program helps in the personal and professional development of both the mentor and the mentee. In contrast, the induction and peer mentoring help the organizations to manage postmerger stress, and provide an opportunity for mentees to familiarize themselves with how different departments and teams work. Senior executives use induction mentoring to reinforce the strategic objectives of the organization. Peer mentoring, in contrast, is focused on how to perform day-to-day activities. The peer mentoring helps new colleagues to ease into the job, and hence reduces the learning curve for the officers. It provides much-needed solace and friendship under the new structure. But in the case of a merger of equals, peer mentoring can create tension among colleagues from different organizations when the processes and procedures are streamlined after the merger, because staff members learning the processes and procedures from their peers might resent it.

In the arrangement where external coaches provide mentoring for senior executives, this helps in bringing out-of-sector experience to solve strategic issues by incorporating and adapting ideas from other business sectors. This further enhances confidentiality, which might be critical in having a competitive advantage. Hence, senior executives receive mentoring to find innovative solutions to the issues faced by their organizations. External coaches provide mentoring to some of the senior executives to help them effectively manage organizational change, or to rediscover a strategic vision and perspective in a rapidly changing business environment. The advantages of this out-of-sector mentoring include innovative ideas, entrepreneurial acumen, and reflective space. However, this mentoring is most suitable for senior executives who are taking their organizations through transformational change. As the industry-specific experience of external coaches might not be up to date, there appears to be a gap in this as well as the industry-specific mentoring programs for senior executives seeking mentoring.

In mentoring the under-represented or disadvantaged groups, the organizations show their care for the communities they serve. This has a positive impact on both the mentor and the mentee, as the organizations are appraised for such initiatives locally and nationally. Such praise and recognition helps in raising the profile of the organizations. These initiatives could help in attracting additional grant funding for mentorship opportunities, which would ultimately lead to a reduction in unemployment-related crimes. As social events and award ceremonies are held at the successful completion of mentoring programs, there is an indication that many organizations are involved in offering similar programs but perhaps not all empowerment mentoring programs are appropriately publicized.

Mentoring programs in this chapter are different from the five mentoring models presented by Patel et al. (2011). Mentoring programs specifically designed for trainee surgeons are difficult to replicate in the transformational change-related business environment. Trainee surgeons have similar professional qualifications at the time of mentoring, whereas mentees within business settings cover a diverse range from unemployed or under-represented groups to senior executives. It can be said that all mentoring programs can benefit an organization; however, two mentoring programs, (1) out-of-sector contract mentoring and (2) induction and peer mentoring, are specifically used to deal with transformational change and postmerger integration.

CHAPTER 5

Coaching in Transformational Change

Introduction

In the previous chapter, we discussed the use of mentoring in managing change to ensure the swift integration of staff after the merger and to enhance the employability of under-represented groups. All forms of mentoring discussed in the previous chapter are used in a positive context to develop the mentees. Coaching, on the other hand, have both the positive and negative connotations based on how this intervention is perceived by the organizations and senior executives.

Coaching is used by some organizations to improve the performance of their under-performing managers and executives. In these organizations, coaching has negative connotations, as the recipients are seen as lacking certain skills and capabilities. The context in which coaching is used to prod senior officials as part of their performance management is discussed in the section on performance coaching in this chapter.

Developmental coaching is utilized in some organizations to develop talented staff members. First-time chief executives, as well as some experienced executives who are implementing transformational changes in an organization for the first time, receive coaching for confidence building and to determine the future direction of their organization. Coaching for the confidence building of senior executives is discussed under developmental coaching as well.

Some organizations use team coaching to enhance team cohesion and to cultivate innovative ideas. Team coaching is used in some organizations to bring different teams together to deal with emotionally charged situations after the merger.

Coaching for Underperforming Directors

The "coaching for underperformance" is also referred to as "performance coaching," "coaching for performance management," and "coaching to improve performance." Some organizations view coaching as a cure to improve the performance of the members of staff who are falling short of their organizational targets. In these organizations, there seems to be a stigma attached to coaching. Rather unsurprisingly, staff working in these organizations do not come forward asking for coaching for their continuous professional development. In these organizations, chief executive or senior directors recommend coaching for certain managers and senior staff who are not meeting their targets.

Performance deficit is noted by line managers and senior executives, who then initiate conversations with underperforming managers and persuade them to attend coaching sessions.

> *It is more to the line management responsibility in discussion perhaps with directors that they get to a stage where they were thinking maybe some external help might encourage that person to improve their performance.*

In these cases, the issues affecting the senior manager's performance are discussed, and a plan of action for improvement is agreed between the underperforming senior managers or directors and their line managers. The coaches are normally hired by the line managers in these organizations, who hold very senior positions such as senior director or chief executive.

In organizations, where coaching is used or perceived as a corrective mechanism, the officials will not come forward to request coaching for personal development. Because of this stigma, in organizations where coaching is linked with poor performance, the executives might opt for training, as opposed to coaching for their leadership development.

Some authors, such as Ellinger et al. (2003), Toit (2007), Peterson (2009), and Robinson-Walker (2012) believe that there is a link between coaching and poor performance. Peterson (2009, 127) classed coaching for underperformance or not meeting important expectations, as "performance management" and differentiated it from developmental coaching, which according to him is "forward looking." Bachkirova (2011, 1) started the introduction of her book with this sentence: "coaches often say that their coaching is developmental, but when asked what they mean by this, the answers are always very different." She observed that in some cases, descriptions of developmental coaching are "practically indistinguishable from any other type of coaching." Developmental coaching is discussed in the next section.

In agreement with the findings of Robinson-Walker (2012) that most health care and nurse leaders in the United States still view coaching as a code for an intervention for poor performance, some organizations in the UK have the same view.

In summation, within some organizations, coaching is viewed as an external intervention to help underperforming managers and executives. The examples of underperformance can relate to staffing issues, inadequate staff management, and the inability to provide leadership during organizational change. The use of coaching to deal with performance deficit by some organizations seems to portray coaching as an off-putting prospect for senior officials who might wish to receive coaching for their professional development. For their leadership development, executives choose training and mentoring instead. Senior executives, who perceive coaching as a "corrective mechanism" for their underperforming colleagues, would find mentoring as a valuable intervention for their own leadership development.

In the existing coaching and mentoring literatures, there is no relationship between performance coaching and mentoring. However, in some organizations, performance coaching and mentoring might be inversely related. This potential relationship has to be explored in future studies to inform coaching and mentoring practitioners. Additionally, the use of coaching to deal with under-performing senior executives appears to have been overlooked by scholars in the UK.

Developmental Coaching

In this section, different characteristics of developmental coaching are presented. Developmental coaching is also referred to as: "executive coaching," "senior management coaching," "strategy coaching," "confidence coaching," and "one to one coaching." Coaching can be used for various developmental purposes, such as to enhance leadership potential, to improve financial or entrepreneurial skills, or to boost the confidence of newly appointed senior executives. Some organizations utilize coaching to polish the leadership potential of aspiring managers. Coaching in this context is focused on releasing the full potential of senior officials. Some organizations use coaching to exploit the potential to generate income and to save costs. This can lead to nonprofit making organizations launching a commercial arm.

New processes and procedures are developed and implemented across the merged organizations, or as part of a transformational change, to develop new and efficient ways of doing business. Coaching can act as an enabler of new ways of working.

Many charities and nonprofit making organizations are shifting their financial models to incorporate income-generating initiatives. There is an emphasis on cost reductions and the swift implementation of new working practices after the merger. Senior executives provide leadership to implement change and establish efficient procedures in their organizations and performance and developmental coaching can be used to address organizational needs.

In organizations where coaching is seen positively as a developmental intervention, it forms part of staff development programs, along with mentoring and training options. Some executives experience receiving coaching as part of their management development programs. In some cases, senior executives receive coaching for confidence building. The factors necessitating confidence coaching can vary, but it can be particularly useful for first time appointed chief executives.

When you get the job, the first chief executive job, you don't get a rule book; you don't get anyone telling you what to do.

The first chief executive job of a large organization can be daunting. However, the coaches act as sounding boards and provide a safe reflective environment for first-time chief executives. As the role of the coach is to support and challenge the chief executive in a confidential way, providing them with safe space to talk about the issues, strategies adopted to tackle those issues, and a reflective assessment of what is working and what is not.

Coaching is also used to help executives in determining the future direction of their organizations after the merger. Some newly merged groups change the name and logo in an effort to create a fresh identity, whereas some organizations hold their history precious and do not wish to lose it after the merger. In these cases, logos and names before the merger are kept and installed alongside the new group name and logo on the group websites and correspondence. So after the merger, each organization ends up with two identities: the acquired group identity and their individual premerger identity. This process can be called having an identity within an identity. In these cases, senior executives can benefit from confidence coaching in creating a new organizational culture and a new group identity. Therefore, coaching is used for postmerger acculturation and confidence coaching empowers the chief executives to deal with organizational identity and culture at the postmerger stage.

Added confidence from coaching can help the executives in moving the organization forward and exercising leadership. Coaching can be used by newly appointed chief executives for confidence building or by existing chief executives, to help them introduce a new organizational culture following a merger. Some organizations incorporate coaching to develop leadership talent and to implement efficient working practices and procedures, which can be the start of a coaching culture in these organizations. Coaching is also used for the development of talented managers. Robinson-Walker (2012, 12) used the term "diamonds in the rough" to describe such talent. The coaching culture, according to Boyce and Hernez-Broome (2011), can be used to create a competitive advantage. This can lead to the organizations becoming financially and procedurally efficient.

Boyce and Hernez-Broome (2011) assert that coaching practices are evolving to address the needs of the changing nature of leadership and organizations. Leadership skills can be enhanced by coaching (Trenner 2013): some organizations are incorporating coaching to develop leadership talent, especially for newly appointed first-time senior executives. Fischer and Beimers (2009, 507) noted that the cliché of it being "lonely at the top" could be no more relevant than it was among executives in the nonprofit sector.

The use of confidence coaching to implement new organizational culture or to introduce new postmerger identity seems to be consistent with social identity theory in mergers (Seo and Hill 2005), especially where after the merger, new group identities, and logos are inaugurated. Tajfel (1972, 292) defined social identity as "the individual's knowledge that he belongs to certain social groups, together with some emotional and value significance to him of group membership." By creating a new group identity after the merger while keeping the premerger identities, the senior executives show their support for the importance of emotional belonging for staff.

Team Coaching

Team coaching in this book refers to arrangements where the whole team in an organization receives coaching together. Some of the team coaching themes can include: (1) team coaching to challenge poor performance, (2) coaching for stagnated teams, and (3) coaching for effective teamwork.

Team coaching is indispensable for organizations that aspire to be recognized as champions in their business sector. For example, if an organization aims to be the "Best Company to Work for," understanding the perception of current staff is important. Independent workplace engagement specialists compile employee opinions and identify areas where companies can improve. As part of the Best Company's survey, all staff members are subject to 360-degree feedback. The managers are rated by the teams they managed. This exercise provides the senior executives with an opportunity to assess the developmental needs of the managers.

Face-to-face communication with the managers who receive negative feedback from colleagues is important. The managers are provided with thinking space; they are invited to reflect on their own practice and are challenged when they are not seen as boosting the mood of their colleagues. Feedback from staff members are used as an opportunity to reinforce the organization's vision and to make the managers aware of the need for improvement.

Senior executives have to be crystal clear with underperforming managers, in a nice way, in a respectful way, but tell them straight; what is acceptable and what is not. It is better to be upfront and straight and give them the right message. The managers need to know the situation, so that they can do something to improve.

However, it is not appropriate to leave the managers to their own devices for improvement. Senior management has to organize appropriate developmental interventions to address any behavioral issues. The managers should have the courtesy to be challenged by their colleagues and the confidence to challenge their seniors for any poor or unprofessional behavior. The management development programs include elements of one-to-one coaching to address specific issues, coaching for team integration, and confidence coaching for junior managers.

It should be the responsibility of the coach to work with the teams and individuals to upskill them and make them feel more confident about what they can offer, and how they can respectfully challenge poor performance and poor attitude among the colleagues and the seniors.

Where coaching is initiated following feedback from colleagues, specific behavioral issues should be explored during one-to-one coaching, rather than during team coaching sessions.

Team coaching is used to facilitate innovative ideas among teams in some organizations. Scantiness of innovative ideas can be a potential problem for the organizations going through difficult times.

Well-established organisation that have done things in a similar way for many years and do not really challenge themselves, don't encourage new ideas to drive things forward have an issue with the organisational culture and leadership.

Even well-established organizations, by just maintaining the status quo, can find themselves in a problematic situation. Coaching in these circumstances can help senior officials to challenge their routine working practices and ingrain innovation. Therefore, team coaching is used in some organizations to develop fresh ideas and to embed an innovative organizational culture.

Team coaching is tailored for the developmental needs of different management levels. The developmental needs depended on organizational objectives, an individual's leadership style, and his or her position in the organization and level of self-awareness.

Team coaching improves joint accountability and responsibility. If a coach is hired to develop the whole executive team, the coach will help them to work more effectively as a team. The coach will be looking at challenges they have got, growing a business, managing in a changing environment. How well the executive team work individually and their attitude to take joint responsibility. Team coaching improves the ability of senior executives to work on collective objectives and to embrace accountability.

In the rapidly changing business environment, skills and capability of senior executives has to be complemented with joint accountability. The logistics of team coaching contributes to team integration, as the coachees are spending more time together than before. This proximity aids the elimination of communication barriers.

The senior executives know more about each other, because they get together for their coaching workshops and have informal chats with each other.

As part of the team coaching process, the team members reflect on their practice as members of multiple teams. The thinking space supports reflection and joint accountability, and cohesiveness can be improved by utilizing team coaching after the mergers. To summarize, team coaching is instrumental in bringing dispersed teams together. Team coaching in due course results in the joint exploration of innovative ideas, and enhances team integration. However, in some cases, too much closeness can be counterproductive, this is discussed next.

Too much closeness can be a hindrance to teamwork in organizations where staff members are oversensitive to each other's emotional state and do not want to say anything to hurt someone's feelings at the postmerger stage. Being responsive to the feelings and emotions of colleagues in a supportive way is important to enhance collegiality and improve working relationships, but in some situations this closeness gets in the way of creativity. The executives get on as a team quite well but they do not challenge each other and lack the creative side of confrontation.

Team coaching has a positive impact on the management team of the recently merged organizations. Senior managers do not want to hurt the feelings of their colleagues by challenging each other shortly after the merger. Coaching gives the managers self-belief and confidence to conduct themselves in a productive manner, confront each other to have healthy discussion, not just nice and cozy, but to build that relationship, that trust, by actually talking about the difficult things, by being prepared to be vulnerable with their colleagues.

Understanding and sharing vulnerabilities is more important and productive for team members than shielding and suppressing emotions. Team coaching provides that safe space and confidence to discuss and positively use emotions. The confidence augments self-belief, which is an important gateway for innovative ideas and new breakthroughs. With this confidence comes more of an ability to try new things, to challenge themselves, and to challenge each other. They think it's okay to have new ideas now, to try things.

Team coaching helps the members of multiple teams in understanding and appreciating that in some cases different teams in an organization has conflicting priorities at the operational level. So coaching is used to highlight the mismatch between operational and strategic objectives.

Team coaching also brings senior managers from different departments together, in the sense of looking at strategic issues from each other's perspective.

Some of the data in this chapter come from the views of coaches on the outcomes of their own coaching, so there might be an issue of bias, such as self-promotion and an opportunity to brag about their coaching skills. The coaches explained how they observed changes in the behaviors and working practices of participants from different teams.

In some organizations, only the behavioral imperfections of the senior management team are observed by their juniors, and reported in the form of 360-degree feedback. These behavioral deficiencies are rectified through external intervention, in the form of coaching. A lack of innovation, leading to stagnation within an organization can be an issue. This shows that organizations might benefit from coaching interventions. Senior managers from different teams within an organization meet during the course of coaching, which leads them to work more cohesively. The self-belief from coaching results in healthy confrontation between team members and the confidence to challenge each other and to discuss innovative ideas and new breakthroughs.

To achieve optimal levels of performance, teams ought to have the necessary skills and capability (Morgeson et al. 2010; Jones et al. 2019). Team coaching can create meaningful and lasting change for individual team members, the team as a whole, and the organization that the team serves, according to Anderson et al. (2008). A combination of one-to-one and team coaching was argued for by Haug (2011), as it helps in building trust between the coach and the coachee. Team coaching can be tailored to meet the specific requirements of an organization including improved performance, lasting change, and creating a friendly and trusting environment for the team members.

Team coaching workshops provide an opportunity for managers to reflect on their own practice. Jones et al. (2019) noted growth in the popularity and practice of team coaching. Mulgan and Albury (2003) found that an overwhelming proportion of senior managers' time is spent on dealing with day-to-day issues, and they have very little space to think about alternative ways of delivering the service. Therefore, team coaching provides thinking space. The team as a whole has to learn and develop in the context of its functions in order to enhance team effectiveness (Jones et al. 2019). Matsuo (2018) found that managerial coaching directly influences team learning and individual learning. According to Smolska (2019), a strong coaching culture contributes to improving a team's performance, employee relations, the well-being of employees and customer satisfaction, increasing engagement, productivity and emotional intelligence, developing leadership, lower turnover rates, faster employee adaptation in the context of entering new team roles, faster adaptation in the team as well as the increase in the number of internal promotions and in gross sales.

Seo and Hill (2005) state that joint accountability enhances team integration and can reduce postmerger anxiety. Team coaching helps senior executives to recognize the importance of joint accountability. Senior executives review strategic challenges from each other's perspective. In some cases, they prepare and deliver joint presentations and team briefs.

The theory of dynamic team leadership by Kozlowski et al. (2009) stated that repeated interactions allow team members to support one another, build trust, and generate a shared mental model of team processes. However, they did not take the emotional revolution into consideration. As noted before, dealing with emotions is an important part of team coaching in any organization after the merger. Team coaching addresses and enriches a number of emotions, such as "preparing to be vulnerable" and "talking about emotions and feelings." This illustrates Kiefer's (2002) identification of a range of emotions resulting from mergers, such as frailty and vulnerability.

Role of Coaching After Mergers

There are several areas where coaching can potentially be beneficial for an organization after a merger.

> It could be a number of things ... developing staff, helping staff to be able to change ... new ways of working, as people have been designated to what the new posts are going to be, or people starting in new posts; it could be around working relationships, it could be dealing with change, it could be about developing them into the role or assisting them to make other choices.

The potential contribution described above is in anticipation of the successful implementation of new staff development policies of which coaching would be an integral part. The scope for using coaching in organizations after a merger is fairly broad, and can include areas of staff development, managing change, postmerger restructuring, and exit coaching.

Instead of coaching, some organizations arrange training events in readiness for the merger. *There is an expectation that the quality of staff that are employed by the organization are able to deal with the merger or transformational change.*

The executives are expected to show leadership while dealing with an organizational change. Senior executives, as part of their professional development during various stages of their professional journey normally have attended leadership programs and in some cases, coaching does form part of the leadership programs.

However, to understand coaching one have to experience it, because if someone has just heard about coaching but has not worked with a coach, it is difficult to get the feel for it. One can understand the theory of coaching, but just the impact that it can have, isn't realized until experienced.

Generally, the mergers are not entirely handled by the executives of an organization. There are external consultants who are employed to explore the options and to advise the executives and the board about the possibility of a merger. There are financial due diligence reports about the viability of the potential merger and the risk profile of the potential merger partners. Even to handle the merger process, external consultants, advisors, and negotiators are hired to help the leadership team. However, the human side of the mergers is normally managed by that organizations' senior executives.

The success and failure of a merger depends on the successful integration of staff. So if the leadership development programs equip the senior executives to deal with the mergers, it is imperative to examine the leadership development programs in contexts other than just the merger.

In the next chapter, organizationwide developmental programs are discussed along with the circumstances in which organizations can use these programs. Table 5.1 shows different forms of coaching and mentoring used during some mergers.

There are potential benefits of embedding coaching within leadership development programs after the merger. These benefits include working relationships in the postmerger context, helping senior officials settle into the new roles, and in some cases exit coaching as well. This is congruent with the existing literature. Boyce and Hernez-Broome (2011) argued that integrating coaching with leadership development would provide leaders with the required developmental experiences to incorporate coaching approaches into their leadership styles. With reference to public health professionals, Risley and Cooper (2011) suggested that adding coaching to professional development would enhance the capabilities of the existing and emerging workforce. Whereas, Anderson et al. (2008)

Table 5.1 Coaching and mentoring in mergers

Stage of merger	Coaching and mentoring at different stages of merger
Before merger	One-to-one coaching/executive mentoring for senior executives: to help executives make strategic decisions about potential merger partners
At premerger stage	Training for managers and directors: to prepare them for dealing with staff enquiries and uncertainties, having an open-door policy and listening to the concerns of staff members
During the merger	Communication and ongoing consultation with staff, road shows for staff, group chief executives attending different forums, and answering questions raised by different stakeholders
Postmerger	• Confidence coaching for senior executives: to introduce new group identity • Developmental coaching: to launch income generation/maximization initiatives • Team coaching for managers: for swift postmerger integration

believe that coaching, in essence, is translating insights into meaningful actions. Organizations going through transformational change can benefit by including coaching as part of their staff development policies.

Indistinctiveness of Coaching and Mentoring

The distinction between coaching and mentoring seem to be blurred. Coaches, mentors, coachees, and mentees have different interpretations of coaching and mentoring.

> Coaching and mentoring are labels … people's understanding of it can be different; coaches and mentors use a similar set of skills and the boundaries can overlap.

Unsurprisingly, many coaches and mentors do not describe themselves as a coach or a mentor, but as a coach and mentor. This can give the impression to the potential users of these services that coaching and mentoring are similar, if not the same. In some cases, senior executives responsible for hiring coaches and mentors do not always have a clear distinction between coaching and mentoring either.

The coaches are aware that coaching as a concept is not fully understood by some of the organizations. This is therefore interesting on several levels and gives rise to a number of questions, such as: (1) If the origins of business coaching were traced to the 1980s (Zeus and Skiffington 2005), then why is coaching still a new concept within some organizations? (2) Are the coaching and mentoring labels exploited by the professionals? (3) Would organizations benefit from a clear distinction between coaching and mentoring? (4) How would the advocates of coaching and mentoring fields perceive these findings?

It is evident that the connection between poor performance and coaching portrays coaching in an unfavorable light. Negativity attached to performance coaching along with a lack of clarity between coaching and mentoring might lead to coaching being provided under the banner of mentoring. So in some organizations, coaching might be provided in the name of mentoring. Furthermore, this assertion could explain the popularity of mentoring, which was noted in the previous chapter.

A clear distinction between coaching and mentoring might not have a noticeable impact on organizations going through transformational change, as the required developmental interventions might still be available, albeit in the name of mentoring. But for coaching and mentoring to establish themselves as separate professions, to capitalize on their past success for marketing and branding, and to develop theoretical bases, a clear distinction between coaching and mentoring is of colossal importance.

Summary

In this chapter, I discussed the role of coaching in organizations going through transformational change. Coaching in some cases can have different meanings to the executives who have received it and to those who have not. On the one hand, coaching is seen as an important developmental intervention used to enhance leadership skills, but on the other hand, it is exercised as a management tool to castigate underperforming senior managers. Because of these conflicting perceptions and practices, some executives favor mentoring or training instead of coaching for their professional development. But the situation is generally reversed for team coaching. Team coaching can be used in merged organizations to serve a variety of objectives, such as to generate innovative ideas, to upskill teams, and to view the strategic objective of the organization from each other's perspective.

Interestingly, sometimes team coaching is used to bring different teams together to achieve organizational objectives, but at other times, the role of team coaching is to overcome the togetherness and closeness, which is seen as restraining innovation in the newly merged organizations. I would argue that the underlying objective of all forms of team coaching is to achieve the strategic objectives of the organization. The objectives can include: to improve performance, to generate additional revenue, and to uphold the "Best Company" image of an organization. Team coaching enhances joint accountability, shared responsibility, and provides a venue to discuss and explore fresh ideas.

In organizations where learning and development teams or human resources departments are considering coaching and mentoring to be part of the staff development strategy, the confusion about the definitions of coaching and mentoring might be eradicated. The use of coaching to embed training in organizations is discussed in the next chapter.

CHAPTER 6

Using Coaching to Embed Training

Introduction

Majority of the mergers, acquisitions, and transformational change studies focus on for-profit organizations. The challenges faced by the organizations operating in the third sector deserve attention too. This chapter concentrates on the transformational change programs in the UK housing sector. Coaching and mentoring can be used to embed training. Coaches and mentors were hired to help implement transformational change in some housing associations in the UK. Part of this transformational change included upskilling junior to middle managers and frontline staff. We draw on the experiences and observations of coaches, who used a combination of teaching, training, mentoring, and coaching to facilitate transformational changes in the housing associations. The study found that in certain cases poor transitional practices in the housing associations can lead to merger failures.

The coaches who were tasked to provide training and vocational qualifications found that some housing officials were promoted to the managerial roles based on their experience. These managers did not have formal leadership and management qualifications. The training included elements of teaching, assessment, and development of managerial skills such as delegation and time management. The study found that coaching helped in embedding training in the housing associations.

Transformational change programs were specially designed for the transformation of housing associations and were labeled by the coaches as: "transformational change package," "consultancy support package," and "turnaround package." The main purpose of these programs was to implement an organizationwide change. Because of the similar nature of these programs, and to avoid any confusion, these programs are all referred to as "transformational change programs" for consistency throughout this chapter.

How Coaching Is Used to Embed Training

The training programs were tailored to the specific requirements of the housing associations. In some cases, the executives attached a requirement for the accreditation of the programs or the inclusion of vocational elements. Coaching was used to embed training, confidence building, and problem solving of the housing officials participating in these programs. Coaching was also used to provide self-belief to the housing officials who were required to submit course work assignments as part of the program. In two out of three programs discussed in this study, a vocational qualification for junior managers formed part of the program.

> *[The chief executive] wanted the coach to have experience of working with [academic] qualifications, wanted the ILM [Institute of Leadership Management] programme to be accredited, but very much wanted it to be tailored to the organisation (Coach B).*

Some managers who received vocational qualifications as part of this program did not have any formal management qualifications or professional development experience, according to the participant coaches. These managers had been promoted to managerial-level jobs on the strength of their experience and long service. The course was aimed at improving staff development and achieving the specific learning outcomes required for the vocational qualification award.

> *I think that [it] would be fair to say people in leadership management positions may have come up through the ranks, so to speak, so perhaps started as workers. They had little if any formal development and certainly, you know, the thought of any academic development terrified them (Coach A).*

The training leading to vocational and educational qualifications was organization-specific, and the staff members were encouraged to include real work-related issues as part of the problem-solving exercises. The Institute of Leadership Management (ILM) course covered leadership theory, whereas real-life work examples provided a practical context, as the course was tailored for the housing association.

> *The ILM course has a theoretical underpinning but it has very much been put into a practical sort of language and context and it is tailored completely to that organisation (Coach B).*

The coaches thought that rather than talking about abstract concepts, the participants might find it easier to follow if real issues were used.

> *We wanted to make it real and put that into practice, really (Coach C).*

The vocational qualification seemed to be a combined effort to tackle issues faced by the managers, with the added bonus of an accredited qualification in the end.

> *All of the examples used are their own; they are bringing in some of their own problems, you know what I mean. It is completely tailored but it ticks all the boxes to get the accreditation (Coach B).*

Since the recipients of the vocational qualification had never received continued professional development before, they lacked confidence. The coaches noted that some participants did not feel confident about writing coursework assignments and attempting the examinations, so coaching interventions were used to boost their self-belief and confidence.

> *So another reason for coaching: the coaching was to build confidence in themselves and in their ability to actually do things, like write assignments and pass exams (Coach D).*

This was a fascinating situation because staff had been appointed or promoted to managerial positions on the strength of their experience and capability of doing the job. But the requirement to attend the ILM accredited course comes across as an exercise to authenticate their experience and capability.

> *They saw ... the ILM course as academic (Coach B).*

The course design facilitated the transfer of training into practical use at work, and at the same time encouraged participants to make practical issues part of the training program. The coaches noted that the housing association staff found coaching helpful regardless of their educational background.

> *Coaching is helping, because they are using it to test [their] ideas (Coach E).*

The accreditation element of the ILM leadership qualification appears to have provided the managers with an opportunity to develop their academic skills. The course design and delivery acted as a platform to discuss and find solutions to work-related problems. This could have cemented the importance of attending that course. For some coachees, this was the first time they had received coaching in any context. In these cases, the inclusion of coaching as part of the feedback and support mechanism for the coursework would have acted as an introduction to these developmental interventions.

Coaching Journey Through the Eyes of a Coach

The participant coach provided some insight into how coaching was used by the housing associations to embed training. The coach was commenting on the training journey of middle to senior managers. The managers were part way through the program. The coach observed an element of resistance and resentment about the program:

> *Particularly, the middle to senior middle managers ... this is not something that most of them were wanting to do (Coach B).*

As part of the program, the managers were required to accomplish an academic qualification, attend workshops, and receive coaching. The coach thought that the onerous nature of the program, coupled with a lack of understanding about coaching instigated resistance. The coach observed how the middle to senior managers were feeling and noted their reactions as follows:

> *Coaching particularly, just, what on earth is this? One-to-one discussions about myself and what I am doing? This was just absolutely crazy. Even if they get supervision, this coaching thing was just seen as: why would I do that? (Coach B).*

The coach got over the initial resistance, as the structure and delivery of the program encouraged the managers to bring their work-related issues to the coaching sessions and workshops and get support.

> *[They] are looking for different approaches and techniques that they can use in their management and leadership role, and it is just the combination of the coaching along with having this input through workshops (Coach B).*

The coach acknowledged that the resistance was not fully eradicated, and in some cases, it had turned into light-hearted banter.

> *Some are still very resistant to do it. You know, some are still [saying] 'all this management rubbish' (laughs). They still got some of that, laughing at themselves, thinking of them as being, you know, leaders and managers (Coach B).*

Another reason that the managers were not fully embracing change could be habitual. The resistance to change as observed by Coach B in the same program will now be discussed in more detail.

Most of these managers started as frontline assistants and officers, who are normally the first point of contact for existing and potential tenants in their roles such as housing officers, tenancy support assistants, property maintenance officers, homeless prevention assistants, and community liaison officers. The coach noted that they had been comfortable in those roles. Sometimes they did not fully appreciate their role as managers, and reverted to being operational. This hands-on practice of serving tenants meant that they struggled with time management, prioritization, and delegation.

> *They are used to being so operational, so hands-on, that those are things they don't necessarily need to do in their leadership role; it can still be a challenge to prioritise that. So for them it's not about their resistance (Coach B).*

The struggle to fully embrace the managerial role was noted by another coach as well. The coach pointed out that the managers grappled with the dilemma of whether they were there to provide managerial support and leadership to their teams or a service to their tenants.

> *Obviously, under pressure people move to the type, so ... we are holding their feet a bit to the fire (Coach A).*

Hence, coaching appears appropriate for reinforcing leadership skills.

Nevertheless, Coach B observed that most of the managers were getting used to their new roles; they were more confident. The coaches talked about a nod of approval and a sense of appreciation.

> *[B]ut more and more, they are really taking on the role, talking about what you're doing and appreciating what they are doing (Coach B).*

The vocational qualification, along with coaching, was seen as confidence boosting. The managers were able to comprehend new ways of working, and they were acknowledging it in their coaching sessions.

> *The majority of people in their coaching sessions are saying: I get this, I can see why we have to do this; and I think they can articulate the difference that all this is making to them, particularly in terms of their confidence as managers (Coach B).*

The coach believed that the success of the program was down to supplementing coaching with academic learning and facilitation in the workshops.

> *So to just have had that [coaching] without the context of the leadership programme and without what looked like embedding the learning, sort of safe enough to have the conversations, I don't think we would have got the results that we have (Coach B).*

Since the coaches were part way through the programs, they were able to comment on the effect of the coaching program on the managers themselves and the teams they manage. One of the coaches laughingly said, *"so it should all work well."* The coaches were able to share the cascade effect of the program.

> *What we're doing in some of the coaching is talking about the role of a leader and a manager in [the] support and development of staff. So it had already started because of what the managers were doing, but it has gone to another level because their staff are starting on the development journey as well (Coach B).*

Kyndt et al. (2012) argued that just offering training opportunities to staff is not in itself sufficient without support for learning also being offered. The design and delivery of the vocational programs in the housing associations seem to be using coaching to provide additional support. Coaching was used to underpin theoretical elements of leadership and management courses as well as helping housing officials in finding solutions to the work-related problems. Clarke (2013) warned that the transfer of training to work situations would be ineffective without taking into consideration the workplace environment. The training programs discussed in this study appear to be set in the workplace environment. The problems faced by the housing officials in their day-to-day job formed part of their course work assignments and coaches helped the participants in identifying and overcoming these problems through training and coaching.

There was a notable similarity between the findings of this study and the one conducted by Forde et al. (2013). In an experiential learning program designed for aspiring head teachers, Forde et al. (2013) noted that coaches reviewed the draft course work assignments with the candidates before the final versions were submitted. The confidence coaching provided to the housing officials as part of the training program discussed in this study also included feedback on their draft course work assignments by the coaches.

Managerial skills such as time management and effective delegation can be improved by training and coaching, according to Ehrich et al. (2001). Coaching could be aimed at: reflecting on ones' own assumptions (Zachary 2005), improving self-confidence (Griffiths 2005), and developing a heightened self-awareness and self-acceptance (Grant 2011).

The observations of the coaches in this study indicate that coaching can be used to: help housing officials understand and appreciate their role in the organization, implement a leadership development program, and overcome initial resistance due to fear of failure or fear of the unknown, as was the case with managers embarking on a management qualification.

Transformational Change Programs

The transformational change programs in the housing associations in this study all involved an organizationwide change, a change in the organizational culture and working practices. Coach C described the transformational change programs as follows:

> *The transformational programme is about [changing] the culture and in order for that to work, obviously you have to get all of the organisation to buy it, so you have to work across the whole of the organisation (Coach C).*

The circumstances for the execution of transformational change programs were different for each housing association, and the programs were tailored to cater for the specific transformational needs of the housing associations. In one case, the transformational change program was introduced after the merger of two housing associations to streamline processes and procedures; in another case, it was to overcome financial difficulties in readiness for a potential future merger. These cases are discussed next.

The housing association in the first case was going through an organizationwide change following a merger. The merger in the first instance was initiated to make potential cost savings.

The organisation had gone through big changes; we had got new leaders in the organisation, a mix from the top of the management team down to sort of first-time junior managers. It was around managing change and managing people (Coach C).

The introduction and implementation of new working processes was the main objective of this program. This included the preparation of detailed procedures, and training to accustom staff to these new procedures and to ensure that these procedures were accepted by the whole organization. People management, according to Coach C, included systems training for officers and confidence coaching for managers to enable them to handle the change efficiently.

In another case, the transformational change program was introduced by a housing association that was going through financial difficulty due to a lack of leadership, according to Coach B. The housing association wanted to be an attractive target for future housing association mergers, and in the observation of Coach B, the transformational change was initiated by the interim chief executive.

The chief executive was invited to leave and an interim chief executive came up with a very different approach, and immediately saw that one of the main challenges for the organisation was the leadership in the organisation (Coach B).

The coaches had to win over the support of staff and cater for the developmental needs of staff working at all levels. The transformational change programs in the housing associations mentioned above were brought about to develop all layers of management within the organization. The individual elements of the programs were designed to the specific developmental needs of each managerial group. The key features of these programs were vocational qualifications, coaching, and mentoring for junior to middle managers, and one-to-one coaching for executives.

[The chief executive] commissioned a leadership programme for his executive team [that is, his directors] and himself, and also a leadership programme for the wider management group (Coach B).

The transformational change programs were tailored to the specific requirements of the housing associations, so certain features were different. The experiences and observations of coaches demonstrated that the transformational change programs were instigated by the new chief executives. The former chief executives to some extent were considered accountable for the financial difficulty, which was seen as one of the reasons for change. So these chief executives were either removed as part of the restructure or were invited to leave where the housing association board did not want a restructure. It comes across rather tellingly that the outgoing chief executives in these cases did not envision organizationwide change, even though it was clearly needed:

> *This was a failing organisation ... the senior team was the poor one (Coach E).*
>
> *This organisation ... was an organisation that was in trouble in a number of ways ... financially in trouble; trouble may be too strong a word ... [but] if they didn't do something pretty fast to cut some costs or to make some efficiencies, and also think of ways to generate some revenue, they were going to be in some trouble (Coach B).*

The common features that led the housing associations to such a state that organizationwide transformation was inevitable, in the view of the participant coaches, included:

- The outgoing chief executive had been in the post for a long period.
- The housing associations were under financial pressure.
- A new chief executive initiated the transformational change program.
- The organization was subject to a radical restructure.
- All levels of management participated in the program.

Generally, a long-serving chief executive can be seen as a safe pair of hands, providing stability to housing associations. But it is important to keep up with the pace of rapid changes in the housing sector. The outgoing chief executives did not adapt their policies and practices in the wake of startling challenges faced by their housing associations. Importantly, the deficient and reactive management approach intensified the financial pressure.

[They] had done things in a similar way for many years (Coach B).

Because of government's financial priorities, the housing associations have to contend with a reduction in grant funding. Hence, they are also actively exploring income-generating opportunities to create additional revenues. In contrast, in the housing associations where transformational change was introduced, in the observation of the participant coaches, the outgoing chief executives had not effectively responded to the changing circumstances.

The transformational change programs were initiated by the incoming chief executives. In one of the housing associations in this study, the interim chief executive brought a trusted comrade with him:

He [the interim chief executive] came in with a guy who he was used to working with, who is a project manager. So he was looking at the systems side of things, shaking things up, making the organisation more efficient (Coach B).

Leadership style comes across as the common denominator in the cases discussed here, as the [outgoing] chief executives seemed to have put their housing associations into financial or operational difficulties. In a constantly evolving organizational environment such as housing associations, the leadership skills of executives and managers ought to be regularly developed. It is not surprising that one of the first tasks of the incoming chief executives was to commission organizationwide programs of leadership development.

Challenges in Implementing Transformational Change

The challenges for housing executives to maintain the financial viability of housing associations, to offer a lean and cost-effective structure in the wake of funding cuts and at the same time make money available for large-scale staff development projects, adds to the financial challenge for housing associations. The housing executives who participated in this study did not introduce organizationwide transformational change programs in their housing associations. However, they were aware of transformational change programs being used in some housing associations. Executive E, for example, described these programs as follows:

> *There are a few [transformational change programmes], where part and parcel of it is [an] integrated, personal development plan. [These programmes] are more sophisticated and look into the issues and everything (Executive E).*

However, there was an air of caution regarding organizationwide programs. Executive D, for instance, drew my attention to the need to balance the training and development needs of staff with ensuring the provision of a consistent high-quality service to tenants. Since the transformational change programs are normally delivered during working hours, that would mean providing a skeleton service structure for tenants while staff are on training courses, which was seen as a challenge.

> *You have normal basic day-to-day things, which I think are incredibly important (Executive D).*

Executive E touched on broader challenges, including practical issues in implementing organizationwide programs:

> *I am talking about the ideal and the reality … [of a] business environment … you know, time pressure; and you have got budgetary pressures, competency and skills pressures. You know, to tie all that, you need (laughs) too much resources and staff commitment to do that. Because people don't understand what coaching is. You and I are talking about [a] bigger map … how you get them to support the staff and colleagues and [provide support] among themselves (Executive E).*

However, the coaches seemed to be aware of the financial and resource pressures faced by the housing associations. Managing a transformational change program for all the management and leadership teams has to be cost-effective for the organization.

> *There were so many of them and it was on a limited budget. They needed one-to-one support, they were not confident … this was all new, so … how … what is [the] priority? So we felt, I mean when we talked about it, we felt the priority was actually to maximise the time that they had with the coach. So the only way we could do this, given that they are all over [names a geographical area], we decided to Skype. So you can imagine, [for the coachees] this was all new as well (Coach B).*

Regardless of the challenges discussed above, the transformational change programs were successfully delivered, according to the coaches. In the case of a restructure of a housing association, discussed earlier, Coach E reported:

> *Those people are now very, very successful senior managers in the organisation, which is an extremely high-performing organisation (Coach E).*

In the other case, where the chief executive was invited to leave because of ineffective leadership and poor financial performance, the coach reported interim results, as the 18-month transformational change program was still ongoing.

> *Oh, it turned out for the better, most definitely. You know, the books balanced and are going in the right direction. The organisation is working together far more as an organisation (Coach B).*

Since these observations of the coaches are self-reported, because of the element of potential bias, such as self-promotion, no firm conclusions can be drawn. The challenges in implementing organizationwide transformational changes in the housing associations include: the cost of commissioning these programs while housing associations are facing a reduction in grant funding, the time commitments of staff, when housing associations are using mergers and restructures to become leaner and cost effective, and a lack of understanding about coaching and mentoring among housing officials. This study found that coaches are aware of these challenges; they make efficient use of information technology by using Skype instead of face-to-face contact for geographically dispersed teams, and offer tailor-made and flexible transformational change programs to minimize disruption to the housing associations.

The transformational change programs discussed in this chapter did not show individual growth in isolation or without making a mark on the housing association itself. Therefore, the transformational change programs within the housing associations appear to have attributes of both transformational change and transformative learning.

The literature appears to be silent about transformational change within housing associations in the UK. Furthermore, existing transformational change models do not include the impact of coaching and mentoring in facilitating change. Anderson and Anderson's (2011, 46) change process model is based on the assumption that employees have a dialog among themselves and identify "a new way of being, working and relating to meet the needs of the future state," the leaders trust this wake-up call for change and the whole organization embarks onto a journey of personal and collective discovery process, which leads to inventing a new way of being and operating in the organization. However, the data collected for this study clearly indicates that coaching, mentoring, teaching, and training were used as vehicles for the transformative learning of housing executives and managers, which led to transformational changes in the housing associations.

Summary

In the housing association sector, supplementing academic and vocational programs with coaching helped embed training in practice. Coaching was used to develop managerial skills, such as problem solving, time management, and delegation. Coaching raised awareness, acceptance, and readiness for change, which could be useful in quashing anecdotal perceptions such as "management rubbish" or "another gimmick."

The transformational change programs discussed in this chapter brought together different developmental interventions, such as training, mentoring, and coaching. The versatility and experience of external coaches required for the delivery and facilitation of these transformational change programs was also emphasized. These programs were commissioned by the incoming chief executives to incorporate organizationwide changes.

The trigger for change in the housing associations did not emerge from within. It appears that the outgoing leaders did not respond to the organizational-level changes necessitated by external factors, such as a reduction in grant funding. The departure of the chief executive and the appointment of a new chief executive signaled that some radical changes were needed: the new chief executives were the ones who commissioned transformational change programs.

The financial challenges faced by the housing associations were intensified by a lack of visionary leadership. The chief executives of these housing associations did not possess the leadership skills required to steer their organization out of financial difficulties. These financial challenges resulted from a reduction in grant funding across the housing sector. Instead of closing the funding gap by either making efficiency savings or by identifying new opportunities to generate revenues, these chief executives did not respond to the changes and were eventually replaced.

The incoming chief executives addressed the urgency of the situation by commissioning external coaches to deliver organizationwide development. The developmental interventions were multifaceted in nature. Training, mentoring, or coaching, either individually or in combination suited the improvement needs and aspirations of different employee groups. These transformational change programs were, according to this study, spread over a 12- to 18-month period. The longer time frame seems to have helped the housing associations in managing their day-to-day business activities and making staff available to attend the program with minimal disruption.

Poor transitional practices, delays in postmerger integration, disparity between premerger promises and postmerger commitment, infrequent employee consultation about postmerger restructuring, and inattention to the merger-related stress and anxiety can influence the success or failure of housing association mergers.

CHAPTER 7

Time-Line Model 1

In this chapter, a theoretical framework in the form of a time-line model of merger process is presented. This model is divided into four stages (as shown in Figure 7.1): before merger (merger considered but partners not identified), premerger (immediately before a planned merger), during merger, and postmerger. The model consists of different forms of coaching and mentoring discussed in Chapters 4 to 6, timing and intended outcomes of these interventions.

Before Merger

Before merger is the most important but implacable stage of the merger process according to the time-line model. Chief executive officers (CEOs) have to identify merger partners or acquisition targets while maintaining utmost secrecy. As we have seen in Chapter 2, when the regulators, investors, or governments have a whiff of the merger proposal, the

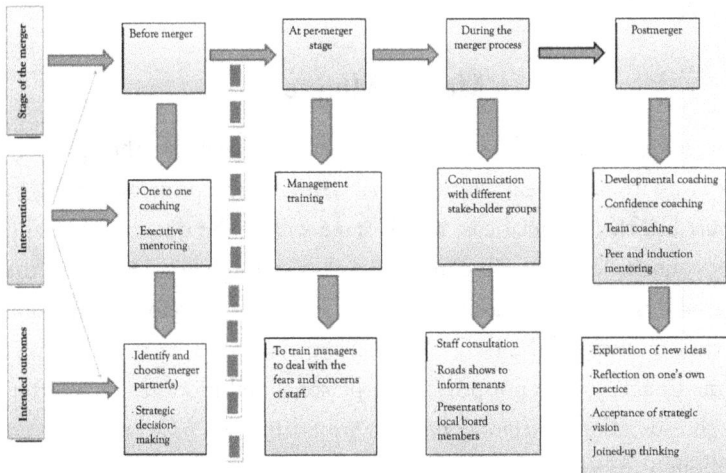

Figure 7.1 Time-line model

organizations involved start getting a lot of unwanted attention. Therefore, commercial sensitivity necessitates that the proposals are discussed with trusted advisors and senior executives in the organization. In the case of a merger of equals, these senior executives might have a vested interest as well. The board structure will change and some of these senior executives might have their job responsibilities downgraded, or they might be invited to leave the organization in the postmerger setup to accommodate merger partners. There is no doubt about the professionalism or quality of advice from senior executives at a risk of losing their jobs, but their attention might be divided between securing their future and concentrating on the future of the organization they are about to leave.

In these situations, CEOs benefit from executive coaching. Executive coaches, who are independent, unbiased, and professionally trained, act as sounding board for CEOs. Executive coaches offer safe space, supportive environment and confidentiality needed to make an important decision. The merger or acquisition decision might be another feather in the cap of a seasoned CEO or a first time experience for a novice CEO. The implications of the decision are far reaching. Therefore, the decision has to be properly thought through. Executive coaches act as critical friends and ask those difficult questions that CEOs might not have thought before or their colleagues might be too scared to ask. Before merger stage questions are divided into two broad categories: Merger motive and Cultural compatibility.

Merger Motive

Before merger stage is also important because any party has the option to walk away from the deal with minimal cost. Yes, the pride or ego might be hurt but the financial cost at this stage will be the due diligence and other consultancy costs. To enter a deal that is in the best interest of the shareholders is the premise of the agency theory. Therefore, evaluating the true motives of the deal and ensuring that the CEOs are delivering the fiduciary duty not pursuing a personal ambition has to be given due consideration. Executive coaches would invite CEOs to reflect on the thought process, ask difficult questions in a friendly environment to get to the bottom of the situation and this process will halt spare of the moment decisions. Because if the decisions are made on past experience without appropriately assessing each situation, the invincibility leads to false sense of infallibility and glaringly obvious issues are trivialized and overlooked.

Merger motive is an important factor when it comes to the infrastructure compatibility. If a company is acquired for strategic reasons such as supply chain management or to have customer access in the areas where the organizations' presence is scattered or nonexistent then infrastructure compatibility is not a deal breaker. The acquired organization can be run with the existing infrastructure as integration would present more problems than solutions. On the other hand, if a merger or an acquisition is motivated by cost savings through streamlining the infrastructure then compatibility must be extensively scrutinized because it is very expensive and in some cases impossible to integrate incompatible infrastructures.

The business structures, processes, assets, and IT systems should be compatible or could be made compatible with relative ease to realize the anticipated synergies. One of the factors in the failure of AOL Time warner merger was the infrastructure incompatibility. In fact, the infrastructures were so incompatible that it was easier and cheaper to develop a new infrastructure than the time and resources required to align the existing ones. If the costs and disruption of infrastructure alignment were factored into the before merger calculations, the deal would not have gone ahead on financial viability grounds.

Executive coaches would invite the senior executives to verbalize the challenges if the potential merger or acquisition proceed. If the senior executives are oblivious to the staff, infrastructure, and cultural integration then difficult questions will be asked. The executives must reflect on the merger motive and integration costs and challenges. Senior executives are generally concerned about the statuary and regulatory requirements, financial and tax structuring, and business synergy challenges. However, the hard fact is overlooked sometimes, that synergies can only be realized with compatible infrastructure.

At the before merger stage, the organizations focus on strategy, synergies, process, and value creation. Teams of advisors, accountants, consultants, and lawyers are hired to address these issues. Such due diligence is crucial to make an informed decision whether to proceed with the deal or not. Due diligence is only effective and useful when senior executives are sincere and open-minded. If the decision has already been made because the CEOs of the concerned organizations believe that "it is a rare opportunity" then due diligence exercise is futile. In Chapter 2, we saw that AOL and Time Warner merger deal was agreed over dinner and due diligence conducted over the weekend. Such due diligence is nothing more than sham tick box exercise. In the case of Bank of America and Countrywide merger, according to some reports, 60 consultants were engaged in the due diligence process but failed to highlight the severity of financial and legal problems. Whether the due diligence teams overlooked these issues or the senior executives involved in the deal chose to ignore the due diligence reports is an important question. Another equally important question is the intent, capacity, and resilience of the due diligence team. Were they influenced by the CEO's tone and belief that the deal was once in a lifetime opportunity and the due diligence reports were prepared under influence? Yet again, the merger motive must be clear from the outset.

Cultural Compatibility

Ruminating cultural differences is vital for the success of a merger or an acquisition. Cultural incompatibilities are not quantified, financial losses because of the cultural gulf, or the consultancy costs to bridge this cultural gulf are not pertinently factored in the due diligence process. Senior executives who ignore the cultural differences do so because they are unfamiliar with the power of emotional intelligence. Because of the training, experience, personality, or financial rewards, senior executives generally find it easy to adapt to a different organizational culture or at least tolerate and work with it. It is a common fallacy that everyone else in the organization has similar personality traits or attitude toward a new organizational culture.

One of the roles, the executive coaches can play at the before merger stage is to check the understanding of senior executives about organizational cultures. History shows that organizational culture can be a deciding factor between the success and failure of a merger. Yet, the history has repeated itself so many times and cultural incompatibility is still overlooked in the mergers and acquisitions that end up failing.

In the case of an international merger or acquisition, cultural compatibility is even more complex. In addition to the organizational cultural differences, the merger partners have to be mindful of the national cultural norms as well. For examples, the cultural aspects of the organizations operating in the United States, UK, Germany, China, and Japan are completely different. In the closed culture countries, because of the bureaucratic processes and regulatory requirements, large-scale merger or an acquisition might not be an option. For example, Japanese distribution system is very fragmented and international organizations are unable to feasibly establish a direct presence; hence, conduct their business through joint ventures or business alliances. Attitudes toward cost savings and adjusting profit margins during downturn can vary as well.

This does not mean that mergers with international or culturally divergent national organizations should not be considered. Each and every merger or acquisition has to be evaluated on its own merits. However, if different cultures, nations, or organizations are involved then the potential delays and reduction in cost savings should be factored into the calculations to assess financial viability.

Ultimately, the objective of entering a merger or an acquisition is that the deal is in the best interest of the shareholders and consumers of previously independent companies. However, if human factors, cultural differences, local customs, national values, and staff attitudes do not form part of the due diligence process then the CEOs are making a decision based on financial figures by ignoring the soft emotional issues. These soft issues are powerful enough to blow apart any deal that is just based on hard facts.

In conclusion, before entering a merger agreement, senior executives have to make strategic decisions about the future of their organization. The right choice of merger partner is extremely important. The incentives and promises have to be assessed by taking into consideration the history, reputation, and motives of the potential merger partners. Based on the commercial sensitivity, peer coaching or mentoring are not appropriate at a strategic level. Senior executives can trust the independence and professionalism of external coaches. Coaches can offer one-to-one coaching or executive mentoring to the senior executives to enable them to make informed and impartial decisions. Coaches act as sounding boards, cultural auditors, and critical friends for senior executives seeking potential merger partners.

The decision to merge affects the lives or livelihoods of a variety of stakeholders, including existing and potential customers, staff, suppliers, subcontractors, and other organizations in the supply chain. So, a clear and transparent merger decision is vitally important. Finding the right merger partner can take a long time. But on balance, it is better to wait for the right merger partner than making a hasty, ill-informed, irrational decision. History of failed mergers and acquisitions has repeated itself over and over again. You don't want to be the one who learnt nothing from history.

Premerger Stage

The premerger stage is distinct from the "before merger" stage. The negotiations, consultations, and due diligence analysis are private and confidential before the deal is signed. Particulars of the deal start becoming public when the deal is concluded and relevant regulatory authorities informed about it. The premerger stage in this model starts after the formal merger agreement has been reached. At this stage, the decision is communicated to all staff members via intranet announcements, staff newsletters, and at employee road shows. Both merger partners carry on serving their customers as normal but start planning the logistics of the merger. To understand the operational practices of the merger partners, reciprocal site visits are arranged. In some cases, exchange staff secondments are also organized to enhance a smooth transition. Communication, consultation, and cultural awareness are important at this stage.

Communication

Timing, text, and tone of the merger or acquisition announcement leaves a lasting impact on staff. Senior executives are generally consulted during the due diligence process even if not directly involved in negotiating the deal. Operational managers, senior managers, and frontline staff are not supposed to know and normally don't know before the deal is formally announced. Senior executives must ensure that staff find out about the deal from the senior management at the first available opportunity. If staff find out about the deal from media or other sources, they would feel being betrayed. Text of the announcement should resonate with staff. Even though the deal might be in the best interest of the shareholders and source of pride for senior executives, the fact remains that the success of the deal is directly related to a lot of frontline and backroom staff losing their jobs. At the same time, senior executives announcing the deal must contain their euphoria and adjust the tone appropriately.

If an organization is stuck in the rut, the investment in resources or talent development is not forthcoming or the regulators have identified operational shortcomings then staff might be relieved if that organization is taken over by a forward looking and financially sound acquirer. Historically, the employees of the acquired organization are more at risk of losing their job. In a merger of equals, to eliminate overlap, some staff from both organizations will be made redundant. Therefore, senior executives must demonstrate emotional intelligence when making the announcements.

It is useful to have the management structure laid out when the merger or acquisition deal is announced. The whole purpose of the exercise is to implement a lean and efficient setup to save costs and maximize profits. But the communication must focus on listening to the fears and concerns of staff and the management must try to address the concerns and allay the fears in an honest manner. If the staff concerns are ignored and the management keeps banging on the new management structure, nobody will pay attention to that. At the same time, if management uses manipulation and coercion to sugarcoat the potential redundancies then it will face resistance, lose credibility, and any cooperation from the affected staff.

Communicating the management structure in the interim is important for the day-to-day running of the business during a period of disruptive change. Without this, the decision makers will not get the information they need to make a timely decision. Quickly placing right people in the interim management and supervisory roles clarifies the reporting lines and to some extent, focuses the mind of staff on external issues. Losing external focus is one of the biggest risks that adversely affects staff and customers. These middle managers and supervisors play a critical role in early days as they are on the floor every day, working, listening, and communicating with employees. Open and timely communication helps talent retention. Prolonged uncertainty, poor communication, and a lack of transparency can lead to the most qualified people leaving first. The lack of communication and coordination can also affect positions further down the hierarchy, when senior managers leave, the uncertainty spreads and the senior management is left without right talent and experience to manage and supervise teams. This affects overall productivity and morale. Therefore, communication is paramount for staff and customer retention.

Consultation

In addition to honest and transparent communication, it is important to engage in an open and frank consultation with all staff at this premerger stage. In the countries and organizations where staff are unionized, the workers unions are consulted frequently at the premerger stage. Where the union culture does not exist, staff representatives, team leaders, and supervisors are invited for consultation for early reassurance, to minimize the disruption and discuss new organizational structure. Consultation helps staff understand the larger goals of the combined organization, and where they fit in that strategy. Some over ambitious CEOs go straight for the cull and start marking staff redundant, to get on with the business of saving costs instead of investing resources in consultation. Staff reduction is expected in all mergers and acquisitions, but if conducted ruthlessly without consultation, haphazardly and without humility and compassion, it will adversely affect the morale of remaining staff, the services they provide to the customers and brand name. Once staff see their colleagues mistreated when they are most vulnerable and powerless, the antimanagement sentiment turns into resentment and even hatred.

Instead of rushing to deliver postmerger cost savings and losing your most important asset, talent along the way, senior business leaders have to change the postmerger dynamics. If postmerger staff reduction is part of the calculations, which mostly is, then the organizations have to move away from postmerger short termism. It will be a lengthy exercise, but senior management must bind their operational managers to organize one-to-one conversations with all staff working in their departments. This exercise will help them understand the motives, pressures, preferences, and ambitions of staff. From that, depending on business needs, the managers can where appropriate persuade experienced staff to stick along for a bit longer and help develop the teams under new structure by sharing their knowledge, experience, and technical skills. At the same time, ambitious staff who can add value to the postmerger setup can be reassured about potential pathways for the career development of these staff members. Some organizations hire independent consultants for screening and assessment of all staff from both merging organizations. This independent assessment helps senior management in making an informed business decision about who stays and who leaves. This might sound as an unpopular proposition but can have a huge impact on the loyalty, commitment, and contribution of staff if they feel that the care and compassion from the management is genuine.

Cultural Awareness

Companies do have different cultures, and reconciling cultural differences are an important part of integration. Cultural difference can include collaboration, communication, participation, promotion, compliance, and coordination. Both parties involved in a merger or acquisition should have a solid understanding of their organizational cultures and the strengths and weaknesses of these cultures. Cultural awareness initiatives soon after the merger or acquisition announcement, gives staff from both parties the opportunity to know more about the daily routines, operational responsibilities, reporting mechanisms, and standard procedures followed by their new colleagues.

Human resources departments can organize reciprocal job shadowing and secondments for a better understanding of the processes adopted on both sides. On one hand, such a move can help staff put things in perspective and know that other colleagues have a shared emotional experience, but on the other hand, this can result in heightened personal anxiety if staff find themselves out of depth with the procedures adopted by their new partners. This might further intensify resistance to change. Fear of the unknown and uncertainty about the future are main reasons for resistance to change in postmerger integration. Resistance is a reaction of the employees, but it can be managed by support from the human resources department and participation in cultural awareness activities with new business partners.

Premerger stage is really a disturbing experience for most staff, who might be required to quickly adapt to unfamiliar policies, practices, and politics; work with former competitors and even strangers. These new colleagues, during the merger process would become competitors again under the new structure, fighting for the same jobs. Staff might have to report to the new managers and supervisors who have very little knowledge of or interest in their past achievements and future ambitions.

The cultural issue is even more prevalent in international mergers and acquisitions. In these cases, organizations have to adapt to local ways of doing things. Try to understand the local culture, or at least be willing to learn about it before making any corporate changes.

The model does not include any form of coaching or mentoring at this stage of the merger. Human resources departments must offer training, advice, and reassurance to enable staff to deal with the fears and concerns. Furthermore, senior management must organize for the thorough assessment of postmerger talent pool to determine the scope of strengths and abilities. This exercise will help organizations to evaluate the cost synergies required to deliver a value-added transition. Communication during mergers and acquisitions is critical. The contribution of public relations, media teams, and human resources departments is important at this stage. But the most important is the conduct and attitude of senior executives in their handling of emotionally charged, fearful, unmotivated, confused, and stressed work force. The workforce seeks clarity on facts, figures, and the future; their own future as well as the future direction of the organization. The care, compassion, and cultural awareness of senior executives, along with holistic approach to communication, consultation, cultural integration, and talent retention, must be discernible at this stage.

CHAPTER 8

Time-Line Model 2

In the previous chapter, before merger and premerger stages were discussed. Now we move on to the during merger and postmerger stages of the time-line model of merger process.

During the Merger Stage

The "during merger" stage is the most chaotic, as at this stage reality hits home. Communication and consultation started at the premerger stage, continues. The executives manage a transformational change while trying to keep the disruption to customer services to a minimum. Senior executives convene meetings with staff groups to explain the decision and to reassure them about the quality and consistency of customer services. At the same time, the senior executives have to deal with staff morale and convince them to carry on offering the same high-quality service. Staff morale is lowest at this stage of the merger.

Communication in some cases becomes a mechanism to vent the frustration and to allay the fears. Both sides, senior management implementing the change and staff affected by the change, feel that their message is not being heard. Senior executives continue reminding staff that they are aware of the disruption and change is necessary for the organization. They make themselves available to answer questions. Staff find that the answers to the questions asked fall short of reassurance. For the questions, like "will my job profile change," "will I have to relocate," "will I even have a job at the end of this integration process?" Management clearly are not in a position to answer these questions. If the questions are not answered in a satisfactory manner, the concerned staff members sometimes conclude that the "management has something to hide." They may see the staff consultation and engagement exercise as sham.

Senior executives understand the stress and uncertainty experienced by staff members, but they maintain that some of the questions relate to the postmerger restructure, which will be finalized at a later stage in consultation with the merger partners. Therefore, even the executives may not know the answers to those questions. This can lead to all sorts of interpretations and rumors. In addition, the nature and frequency of questions can change on a daily basis depending on what staff members hear from each other and who they choose to believe. Senior executives have to concentrate on the merger process and cannot engage in staff consultation on a daily basis. The unanswered questions and the inherent uncertainty add to the mistrust between staff and senior executives.

Operational managers are rarely consulted in the merger process, but are made responsible and accountable for the standard of service without providing additional resources, in most cases with fewer resources. As staff take early retirement or resign to move on to other jobs, the vacancies are not filled straight away because the postmerger organization structure is not finalized. Customers expect more but organizations fail to adapt business practices to shifting expectations and this sends out a wrong message. Some experienced staff members who do not want to go through the uncertainty take early retirement or change jobs. New staff members are not recruited because of the time delay in finalizing postmerger organizational structure. Some staff members go on stress-related sick leave.

Some organizations bring a team of experienced professionals to handle the integration process. Operational managers report to these integration specialists. To some extent this allows operational managers to focus on day-to-day running of their departments while the change-related issues are handled by specialists. However, these specialists are seen as "parachuters" with little knowledge or understanding of the work and contribution of individual staff members. Nevertheless involving specialists does bring some order and normality to the otherwise disruptive and chaotic environment.

Coffee machines, photocopiers, and quiet corners in the staff canteen are used to share the gossip and rumors as well as an opportunity by managers to provide some between the lines reassurance to key staff members. Words to the effect *"you should not worry," "I think your job is safe,"* and so on are whispered to some staff members. Nevertheless, these reassuring messages come with a caveat "of course, I am not in a position to offer 100% guarantee, because it depends on the final restructure." As these "quiet words" do not provide cast iron guarantee, staff remain anxious and nervous. However, this constant communication is important to avoid paralysis and to maintain morale.

As postmerger structures are finalized in various departments, surplus staff start leaving. Senior executives and operational managers must treat these staff members with dignity, respect, and support they deserve. These people are not only losing their jobs but also long-standing friendships and social connectedness are affected. The leavers go through a range of emotions, including anger, pain, confusion, and disillusionment. Unless they are in a position to find an alternative employment fairly quickly, their self-esteem becomes precarious leading to powerlessness, depression, and fear. Therefore, senior management have to adopt a caring and considerate approach. Not only because this approach is the humane thing to do but also to send a positive message to other staff that their friends and former colleagues are respected and supported.

Coaching or mentoring during the merger process stage are not used for the following reasons: (a) staff availability: fewer, overworked, stressed staff members are responsible for delivering day-to-day services, hence cannot be made available to attend coaching or mentoring sessions, (b) the element of mistrust discussed earlier, (c) the focus of the management is to deliver the merger within a set timescale, so staff development at this stage is not a priority, and (d) coaching or mentoring might not provide the answers sought by staff members.

Postmerger Stage

Coaching and mentoring in various forms can be used by the organizations at the postmerger stage. One-to-one coaching and executive mentoring for the development of first time directors following the postmerger restructure, confidence coaching for senior executives wishing to implement a new organizational culture, team coaching to foster joined-up thinking and to manage emotional sensitivity, induction mentoring to infuse organizational values, peer mentoring to support staff through the changeover and a combination of coaching and mentoring interventions as part of transformational change programs. For a merger to be successful, the executives must have a clear understanding of their customers and clients, develop procedures, and train staff to serve the customers.

To implement rearranged reporting and redesigned business processes, it is vital that staff are fully trained and have the supervisory support mechanism for the prompt resolution of any teething problems. There is a risk that staff might revert to the old way of working because of lack of clarity, cumbersome procedures, training deficiencies and inadequate follow up, and postimplementation audit. Staff members can be given the ownership of change, by involving them in developing new processes and reporting mechanisms. Developmental needs identified can be met through training, development, coaching, mentoring, and other interventions. However, at the end of this process, all staff members have to take responsibility for the implementation of the changes, relevant to their job profile. Root causes for any noncompliance must be established and swift corrective action must be taken.

Human resources departments have a role to play as well. With the new organizational structure, new job profiles, and specifications should be created to reflect the new structure. Staff appraisals, annual reviews, and other performance evaluation criteria should be aligned. Human resources department should articulate the strategy and cultural values of the newly merged organization, up and down its corporate structure. Effective implementation of processes and procedures can prevent merger failures.

The difference between a full merger failure and partial merger failure can be influenced by the level of postmerger integration. If the merged organizations keep running their premerger operational systems in parallel for logistical or technological reasons, then postmerger integration is minimal. Running premerger operational systems in parallel does not deliver cost savings and anticipated synergies but it does give the management strategic flexibility of a smooth and nondisruptive demerger in future. On the other hand, if the motive or circumstances of the merger do not require demerger flexibility, then postmerger integration at all levels is vital. Without that, merger or acquisition will be a failure. Therefore, a greater focus on postmerger integration can reduce merger failures.

The importance of cultural differences and the distinctiveness of the social identities of employee groups pose a potential threat to the success of a merger. Coaching and mentoring play an important role in the initiation, execution and management of acquisitions, mergers and transformational changes. Coaching and mentoring can have an impact on the success or failure of a transformational change if it is used for staff and systems integration at the postmerger stage. Coaching and mentoring can lead to smooth postmerger staff integration. Confidence coaching can help in creating a new shared identity for the merged organizations. One-to-one executive coaching and executive mentoring are used by the chief executives to explore viable alternatives, potential merger partners, and the impact of the merger on customers.

Mergers and transformational changes intensify emotional sensitivity among staff at all levels but this affects individuals in different ways. Team coaching is used to deal with contrasting emotional situations that result from the mergers. It is not unusual for staff to try to suppress their emotions, stick together with their premerger colleagues, and not fully embrace the postmerger team structure. At the same time, some staff members can become oversensitive and avoid full and frank discussions on thorny issues such as postmerger team structures and budgetary allocations.

A symbolic yet emotionally powerful strategy is the creation of a new group identity for all the merged organizations within the group. A new group name and a new group logo jointly developed and adopted by the merged organizations can ease the postmerger integration. Yet, at the same time, premerger names and logos are also kept and installed side by side with the new logo. By maintaining the existing identity of all staff by keeping the names and logos, it is ensured that their social identity is not lost, while at the same time, a new group identity is introduced. This "dual identity" or "an identity within an identity," contributes to the success of the merger. Therefore, success of a merger can be linked to the swift transition and effective management of human factors.

Team coaching is used to overcome these different situations that result from emotional sensitivity. In some departments of the same organization, team coaching might be used to bring different team members together, to enable them to see things from each other's perspective, and to work together as a team. Whereas in another department, the team coaching might be used to encourage healthy confrontation and challenge, if emotional sensitivity is seen as restraining innovation.

Team coaching in the merged organizations facilitate repeated interactions among staff. Repeated interactions are crucial elements of the theory of dynamic team leadership. However, these interactions are hard to accomplish soon after the merger, because it is common for organizations from different cities, states, or even countries to merge. It takes time to move to a central postmerger group head office because of the logistics, the contractual obligations such as leases, and the amount of time taken to establish a new organizational structure.

Team coaching can bring senior managers from different departments into physical proximity, enabling face-to-face meetings with their counterparts when attending team coaching sessions. This helps in discussing some issues face-to-face rather than over the phone or via e-mail. Therefore, team coaching sessions can provide repeated interactions for geographically dispersed teams. Furthermore, members of multiple teams can be coached together to enhance joint accountability and cohesiveness by being provided with reflective space in a supportive environment. It enhances team effectiveness; empowers teams to generate results; and adopts appropriate approach for creating lasting change. Team coaching can be used to mollify emotionally charged situations as well as to kindle difficult conversations among team members after a merger.

On a practical level, the diverse range of human emotions following the merger needs to be recognized by senior executives. The issues underlying emotional sensitivity should be explored and addressed in a compassionate and supportive environment by professional coaches. However, there is generally an air of caution regarding organization-wide programs. Senior executives have to pay attention and balance the training and development needs of staff while ensuring the provision of a consistent high-quality service to customers. Since the transformational change programs are normally delivered during working hours, that would mean providing a skeleton service structure for customers while staff are on training courses, is a challenge. In addition, chief finance officers might think mergers to be a business decision, driven by the organizations' strategic vision. The "cost" of providing coaching and mentoring must justify the "value" it adds to the merged organizations.

Managing a transformational change program for all the management and leadership teams is a real balancing act for the coaches too. The coaches would like to provide as much help and support as required by the coachees, but they have to make a decision about face-to-face contact time versus other modes of support. One option can be to deliver one-to-one coaching for the executive team and face-to-face vocational qualification workshops for junior to middle managers, whereas additional coaching support via virtual means.

Magnitude and frequency of changes in many organizations is fascinating. The transformational change programs discussed in this book do not show individual growth in isolation or without making a mark on an organization itself. Therefore, the transformational change programs have the attributes of both transformational change and transformative learning.

A coach and a mentor understand the importance of human factors and the stress and anxiety caused by the mergers. However, it is easy to underestimate the intensity of human emotions at play during the merger process. On the one hand the emotional sensitivity brings employees closer together, but on the other hand the commissioning of coaching and mentoring can be seen by staff with mistrust and called a "management gimmick."

This time-line model provides the practitioners (coaches, mentors, and trainers) with evidence on which to base their services and provides researchers with an opportunity to develop a formal theory. This model enables coaches to reflect on their own practice, how coaching and mentoring are used in organizational mergers and acquisitions and how the time-line model can be integrated into their coaching and mentoring services.

Abbreviations

Chapter 2
PMI, Philip Morris International
FDA, Food and Drug Administration
CEO, Chief Executive Officer
CDMA, Code Division Multiple Access

Chapter 4
NEW, Network of Executive Women
TMP, Toyota Mentorship Program

Chapter 6
ILM, Institute of Leadership Management

References

Alhamami, N.M., W.K. Wan Ismail, S. Kamarudin, and F.Z. Abdullah. 2020. "Linking Emotional Intelligence and Transformational Leadership to Job Performance in a Conflict-Stricken Environment." *Journal of Talent Development and Excellence* 12, no. 3s, pp. 2153–2163.

Anderson, A.L., and D. Anderson. 2001. *Beyond Change Management: Advanced Strategies for Today's Transformational Leaders.* San Francisco: Jossey-Bass/Pfeiffer.

Anderson, M.C., D.L. Anderson, and W.D. Mayo. 2008. "Team Coaching Helps a Leadership Team Drive Cultural Change at Caterpillar." *Global Business and Organizational Excellence* 27, no. 4, pp. 40–50.

Arango, T. January 10, 2010. "In Retrospect: How The AOL-Time Warner Merger Went So Wrong." *The New York Times,* Available at www.nytimes.com/2010/01/11/business/media/11merger.html (accessed December 16, 2020).

Argyris, C. 1987. "Reasoning, Action Strategies, and Defensive Routines: The Case of OD Practitioners." In *Research in Organisational Change and Development,* eds. R.A. Woodman, and A.A. Pasmore, 89–128. Greenwich: JAI Press.

Argyris, C., and D. Schön. 1978. *Organizational Learning: A Theory of Action Perspective.* Reading: Addison Wesley.

Arthur, L. 2010. *Staff Feelings About a Merger in Higher Education: A Longitudinal Case Study.* [PhD Thesis]. Lancaster University, UK.

Bachkirova, T. 2011. *Developmental Coaching: Working with the Self.* Maidenhead: Open University Press.

Bamford, C. 2011. "Mentoring in the Twenty-First Century." *Leadership in Health Services* 24, no. 2, pp. 150–163.

Bauer, F., D. Degischer, and K. Matzler. 2013. "Is Speed of Integration in M&A Learnable? The Moderating Role of Organisational Learning on the Path of Speed of Integration on Performance. Management, Knowledge and Learning." International Conference 19–21 June 2013 Zaadar, Croatia.

Baugh, S.G., and E.A. Fagenson-Eland. 2005. "Boundaryless Mentoring: An Exploratory Study of the Functions Provided by Internal Versus External Organisational Mentors." *Journal of Applied Social Psychology* 35, no. 5, pp. 939–955.

Beckhard, R. 1969. *Organisational Development: Strategies and Models.* Reading, MA: Addison-Wesley.

Birkinshaw, J., H. Bresman, and L. Håkanson. 2000. Managing the Post-Acquisition Integration Process: How the Human Integration and Task Integration Processes Interact to Foster Value Creation." *Journal of Management Studies* 37, no. 3, pp. 395–425.

Blackman, A.C. 2007. *The Effectiveness of Business Coaching: An Empirical Analysis of the Factors that Contribute to the Successful Outcomes*, [PhD Thesis]. James Cook University, Australia.

Bligh, M.C. 2006. "Surviving Post-Merger 'Culture Clash': Can Cultural Leadership Lessen the Casualties?" *Leadership* 2, no. 4, pp. 395–426.

Bokeno, R.M., and V.W. Gantt. 2000. "Dialogic Mentoring: Core Relationships for Organisational Learning." *Management Communication Quarterley* 14, no. 2, pp. 237–270.

Bóo, M. 2008. "Debate: An Entrepreneurial Public Sector." *Public Money & Management* 28, no. 5, pp. 264–266.

Boyce, L.A., and G. Hernez-Broome. 2011. "Introduction: State of Executive Coaching: Framing Leadership Coaching Issues." In *Advancing Executive Coaching: Setting the Course for Successful Leadership Coaching*, eds. G. Hernez-Broome and L.A. Boyce, San Francisco: Jossey-Bass Wiley.

Brahma, S.S. 2003. "Organisational and Human Resource Related Issues in Mergers and Acquisitions: A Review." *Mergers and Acquisitions*, from http://ICWAI.org (accessed August 18, 2011).

Bresser, F., and C. Wilson. 2010. "What is Coaching?" In Passmore (ed) *Excellence in coaching: The industry guide. Association for Coaching*, 2nd ed. 9–26. London: Kogan Page.

Bruck, C. 2009. "'Angelo's Ashes: The Man Who Became the Face of Financial Crisis'." *The New Yorker*, 22 June. Available at www.newyorker.com/magazine/2009/06/29/angelos-ashes (accessed January 30, 2021).

Buono, A.F., and J.L. Bowditch. 2003. *The Human Side of Mergers and Acquisitions: Managing Collusions Between People, Cultures and Organisations*. Washington: Beard Books.

Burdett, J.O. 1998. "Forty Things Every Manager Should Know About Coaching." *Journal of Management Development* 17, no. 2, pp. 142–152.

Caplan, J. 2003. *Coaching for the Future: How Smart Companies use Coaching and Mentoring*. London: CIPD.

Cartwright, S., and C.L. Cooper. 1993. "The Psychological Impact of Merger and Acquisition on the Individual: A Study of Building Society Managers." *Human Relations* 46, no. 3, pp. 327–347.

Cartwright, S., and R. Schoenberg. 2006. "Thirty Years of Mergers and Acquisitions Research: Recent Advances and Future Opportunities." *British Journal of Management* 17, no. (S1), pp. S1–S5.

Cartwright, S., M. Tytherleigh. and S. Robertson. 2007. "Are Mergers Always Stressful? Some Evidence from the Higher Education Sector." *European Journal of Work and Organisational Psychology* 16, no. 4, pp. 456–478.

Cavanagh, M.J., and A.M. Grant. 2004. "Executive Coaching in Organisations: The Personal is the Professional." *International Journal of Coaching in Organisations* 2, no. 2, pp. 6–15.

Cavanagh, M.J., and A.M. Grant. 2005. *Introduction. Evidence-Based Coaching: Theory, Research and Practice from the Behavioural Sciences.* Brisbane: Australian Academic Press.

Celiktas, M., G. Grayson, N. Mireles, and T. Reid. 2016. "Analysis of a Failed Merger: Sprint-Nextel Case." Naval Postgraduate School – Advanced Financial Reporting, 1-17.

Chandler, D.E. 2011. "The Maven of Mentoring Speaks: Kathy E. Kram Reflects on her Career and the Field." *Journal of Management Inquiry* 20, no. 1 pp. 24–33.

Chapman, J.A. 2002. "A Framework for Transformational Change in Organisations." *Leadership & Organization Development Journal* 23, no. 1, pp. 16–25.

Chatterjee, S., M.H. Lubatkin, D.M. Schweiger, and Y. Webber. 1992. "Cultural Differences and Shareholder Values in Related Mergers: Linking Equity and Human Capital." *Strategic Management Journal* 13, no. 5, pp. 319–334.

Christensen, C.M., R. Alton, C. Rising, and A. Waldeck. 2011. "The New M&A Playbook." *Harvard Business Review* 89, no. 3, pp. 48–57.

Cinite, I., L.E. Duxbury, and C. Higgins. 2009. "Measurement of Perceived Organizational Readiness for Change in the Public Sector." *British Journal of Management* 20, no. 2, pp. 265–277.

CIPD. 2013. "Annual Survey Report: Learning and Talent Development." Available at http://www.cipd.co.uk (accessed June 08, 2013).

Clarke, N. 2013. "Transfer of Training: The Missing link in Training and the Quality of Adult Social Care." *Health and Social Care in the Community* 21, no. 1, pp. 15–25.

Clutterbuck, D. 2008. "What's Happening in Coaching and Mentoring? And What is the Difference Between Them?" *Development and Learning in Organizations* 22, no. 4, pp. 8–10.

Clutterbuck, D. 2012. "Cross-Organizational Mentoring." *David Clutterbuck Partnership*. Available at https://davidclutterbuckpartnership.com/cross-organizational-mentoring/ (accessed November 01, 2020).

Collins, J.M., and C. O'Rourke. 2012. "The Application of Coaching Techniques to Financial Issues." *Journal of Financial Therapy* 3, no. 2, pp. 39–56.

Cox, E. 1999. "Mentors – Born or Made? A Study of Mentor Development in a Community Mentoring Context." [PhD Thesis] Lancaster University, UK.

Cox, E. 2006. "An Adult Learning Approach to Coaching." In *Evidence Based Coaching Handbook*, eds. M. Grant and R. Stober, 193–217. Hoboken, NJ: Wiley & Sons.

Dahl, M.S. 2011. "Organizational Change and Employee Stress." *Management Science* 57, no. 2, pp. 240–256.

Degbey, W.Y., P. Rodgers, M.D. Kromah, and Y. Weber. 2020. "The Impact of Psychological Ownership on Employee Retention in Mergers and Acquisitions." *Human Resource Management Review*, p. 100745.

De Keyser, B., A. Guiette, and K. Vandenbempt. 2021. "On the Dynamics of Failure in Organizational Change: A Dialectical Perspective." *Human Relations* 74, no. 2, pp. 234–257.

D'Ortenzio, C. 2012. *Understanding Change and Change Management Processes: A Case Study.* University of Canberra.

Dougall, D., M. Lewis, and S. Ross. 2018. "Transformational Change in Health and Care: Reports from the Field." *The King's Fund.* www.kingsfund.org.uk

Dutton, J.E., and J.M. Dukerich. 1991. "Keeping an Eye on the Mirror: Image and Identity in Organizational Adaptation." *Academy of Management Journal* 34, no. 3, pp. 517–554.

Dymock, D. 1999. "Blind Date: A Case Study of Mentoring as Workplace Learning." *Journal of Workplace Learning: Employee Counselling Today* 11, no. 8, pp. 312–317.

Ehrich, L.C., B.C. Hansford, and L. Tennent. 2001. "Closing the Divide: Theory and Practice in Mentoring." Paper prepared for ANZAM 2001 Conference, 'Closing the Divide', Auckland, New Zealand.

Ellinger, A.D., A.E. Ellinger, and S.B. Keller. 2003. "Supervisory Coaching Behaviour, Employee Satisfaction, and Warehouse Employee Performance: A Dyadic Perspective in the Distribution Industry." *Human Resource Development Quarterly* 14, no. 4, pp. 435–458.

Evered, R.D., and J.C. Selman. 1989. "Coaching and the Art of Management." *Organizational Dynamics* 18, no. 2, 16–32.

Faghihi, A., and S.M. Allameh. 2012. "Investigating the Influence of Employee Attitude Toward Change and Leadership Style on Change Readiness by SEM (Case Study: Isfahan Municipality)." *International Journal of Academic Research in Business and Social Sciences* 2, no. 11, pp. 215–227.

Fischer, R.L., and D. Beimers. 2009. "Put Me In, Coach': A Pilot Evaluation of Executive Coaching in the Nonprofit Sector." *Nonprofit Management and Leadership* 19, no. 4, 507–522.

Fitzpatrick, D. July 1, 2012. "'BofA's Blunder: $40 Billion-Plus'." *The Wall Street Journal,* Available at www.wsj.com/articles/SB10001424052702303561504 577495332947870736 (accessed January 12, 2021).

Forde, C., M. McMahon, P. Gronn, and M. Martin. 2013. "Being a Leadership Development Coach: A Multi-Faceted Role." *Educational Management Administration & Leadership* 41, no. 1, pp. 105–119.

Fox, R., A. Henderson, and K. Malko-Nyhan. 2005. "They Survive Despite the Organizational Culture, Not Because of it': A Longitudinal Study of New Staff Perceptions of What Constitutes Support During the Transition to an Acute Tertiary Facility." *International Journal of Nursing Practice* 11, no. 5, pp. 193–199.

Gardner, L., and C. Stough. 2001. "Examining the Relationship Between Leadership and Emotional Intelligence in Senior Level Managers." *Leadership and Organisation Development Journal* 23, no. 2, pp. 68–78.

Garrow, V. 2010. *Evaluation of the Academy for Large Scale Change*. Institute of Employment Studies, NHS, UK.

Garvey, B. 2004. "The Mentoring/Counselling/Coaching Debate: Call the Rose by Any Other Name and Perhaps it's a Bramble?" *Development and Learning in Organisations* 18, no. 2, pp. 6–8.

Garvey, B., and G. Alred. 2000. "Developing Mentors." *Career Development International* 5, no. 4, pp. 216–222.

Garvey, B., P. Stokes, and D. Megginson. 2009. *Coaching and Mentoring: Theory and Practice*. London: Sage.

Gegner, C. 1997. *Coaching: Theory and practice. Unpublished Master's Thesis*. University of San Francisco, San Francisco, CA.

Gloss, E.J. 2013. "A Hint of this and a Pinch of that: Theories that Inform Coaching and Consulting." *Graduate Studies Journal of Organizational Dynamics* 2, no. 1, pp. 1–13.

Graham, S., J. Wedman, and B. Garvin-Kester. 1993. "Manager Coaching Skills: Development and Application." *Performance Improvement Quarterly* 6, no. 1, pp. 2–13.

Grant, A.M. 2001. "Towards a Psychology of Coaching: The Impact of Coaching on Metacognition, Mental Health and Goal Attainment." [PhD Thesis], Macquarie University, Australia.

Grant, A.M. 2005. "What is Evidence-Based Executive, Workplace and Life Coaching?" In *Theory, Research and Practice from Behavioural Sciences*, eds. M. Cavanagh, A.M. Grant and T. Kemp, 1–12. Brisbane: Australian Academic Press.

Grant, A.M. 2007. "Enhancing Coaching Skills and Emotional Intelligence Through Training." *Industrial and Commercial Training* 39, no. 5, pp. 257–266.

Grant, A.M. 2011. "Developing an Agenda for Teaching Coaching." *International Coaching Psychology Review* 6, no. 1, pp. 84–99.

Grant, A.M. 2013. "The Efficacy of Executive Coaching in Times of Organisational Change." *Journal of Change Management*, pp. 1–23.

Grant, A.M., and M.J. Cavanagh. 2004. "Toward a Profession of Coaching: Sixty-Five Years of Progress and Challenges for the Future." *International Journal of Evidence Based Coaching and Mentoring* 2, no. 1, pp. 1–16.

Grant, A.M., L. Curtayne, and G. Burton. 2009. "Executive Coaching Enhances Goal Attainment, Resilience and Workplace Well-Being: A Randomised Controlled Study." *The Journal of Positive Psychology* 4, no. 5, pp. 396–407.

Greenwood, R., and C.R. Hinings. 1996. "Understanding Radical Organizational Change: Bringing Together the Old and the New Institutionalism." *Academy of Management Review* 21, no. 4, pp. 1022–1054.

Griffiths, K. 2005. "Personal Coaching: A Model for Effective Learning." *Journal of Learning Design* 1, no. 2, pp. 55–65.

Guillemin, M., and L. Gillam. 2004. "Ethics, Reflexivity, and 'Ethically Important Moments' in Research." *Qualitative Inquiry* 10, no. 2, pp. 261–280.

Gyllensten, K., and S. Palmer. 2005. "Can Coaching Reduce Workplace Stress? A Quasi-Experimental Study." *International Journal of Evidence Based Coaching and Mentoring* 3, no. 2, pp. 75–85.

Gyllensten, K., and S. Palmer. 2006. "Experiences of Coaching and Stress in the Workplace: An Interpretative Phenomenal Analysis." *International Coaching Psychology Review* 1, no. 1, pp. 86–98.

Hackman, J.R., and G.R. Oldham, G.R. 2005. "How Job Characteristics Theory Happened." In *The Oxford Handbook of Management Theory: The Process of Theory Development*, eds. K.G. Smith and M.A. Hitt, 151–170. Oxford: Oxford University Press.

Hackman, J.R., and R. Wageman. 2005. "A Theory of Team Coaching." *Academy of Management Review* 30, no. 2, pp. 269–287.

Hamlin, R.G., A.D. Ellinger, and R.S. Beattie. 2008. "The Emergent 'Coaching Industry': A Wake-Up Call for HRD Professionals." *Human Resource Development International* 11, no. 3, pp. 287–305.

Hart, K. November 24, 2007. "No Cultural Merger At Sprint Nextel." *The Washington Post*, Available at www.pressreader.com/usa/the-washington-post/20071124/282467114546044 (accessed January 30, 2021).

Hatmaker, D.M., H.H. Park, and R.K. Rethemeyer. 2011. "Learning the Ropes: Communities of Practice and Social Networks in the Public Sector." *International Public Management Journal* 14, no. 4, pp. 395–419.

Haug, M. 2011. "What is the Relationship Between Coaching Interventions and Team Effectiveness?" *International Journal of Evidence Based Coaching and Mentoring*, no. 5, pp. 89–101.

Henderson, G.M. 2002. "Transformative Learning as a Condition for Transformational Change in Organizations." *Human Resource Development Review* 1, no. 2, pp. 186–214.

Heslin, P., J.B. Carson, and D. VandeWalle. 2009. "Practical Applications of Goal Setting Theory to Performance Management." In *Performance Management: Putting Research into Action,* eds. J. Smither and M. London, 89–114. San Francisco: Jossey-Bass.

Hezlett, S.A., and S.K. Gibson. 2005. "Mentoring and Human Resource Development: Where We are and Where We Need To Go." *Advances in Developing Human Resources* 7, no. 4, pp. 446–469.

Hubbard, N. 2001. *Acquisition Strategy and Implementation,* Revised ed. Basingstoke: Palgrave.

Hudson, F.M. 1999. *The Handbook of Coaching.* San Francisco: Jossey-Bass.

International Coach Federation. 2007. "The ICF Definition of Coaching." *In the ICF Codes of Ethics.* Available at www.coachfederation.org/ICF/ForþCurrentþMembers/EthicalþGuidelines (accessed April 05, 2012).

Issah, M. 2018. "Change Leadership: The Role of Emotional Intelligence." *SAGE Open* 8, no. 3, p. 2158244018800910.

Jacobson, S.L., and D.R. Sherrod. 2012. "Transformational Mentorship Models for Nurse Educators." *Nursing Science Quarterly* 25, no. 3, pp. 279–284.

Jansson, N. 2013. "Organisational Change as Practice: A Critical Analysis." *Journal of Organisational Change Management* 26, no. 6, pp. 1003–1019.

Jarrett, M. 2003. "The Seven Myths of Change Management." *Business Strategy Review* 14, no. 4, pp. 22–29.

Jarvis, J., D.A. Lane., and A. Fillery-Travis. 2006. *The Case for Coaching: Making Evidence-Based Decisions on Coaching.* London: CIPD.

Jemison, D.B., and S.B. Sitkin. 1986. "Corporate Acquisitions: A Process Perspective. *Academy of Management Review* 11, no. 1, pp. 145–163.

Jones, R.J., U. Napiersky, and J. Lyubovnikova. 2019. "Conceptualizing the Distinctiveness of Team Coaching." *Journal of Managerial Psychology.*

Joo, B.K.B. 2005. "Executive Coaching: A Conceptual Framework from an Integrative Review of Practice and Research." *Human Resource Development Review* 4, no. 4, pp. 462–488.

Kanyangale, M., and N. Pearse. 2012. "Weaving the Threads of Reflexivity: Coming to Terms with Grounded Theory Research." In *Proceedings of the 11th European Conference on Research Methods* (190–198). Academic Conferences Limited.

Kiefer, T. 2002. "Understanding the Emotional Experience of Organizational Change: Evidence from a Merger." *Advances in Developing Human Resources* 4, no. 1, pp. 39–61.

Kotter, J.P. 1996. *Leading Change.* Boston: Harvard Business School Press.

Kozlowski, S.W., D.J. Watola, J.M. Jensen, B.H. Kim, and I.C. Botero. 2009. "Developing Adaptive Teams: A Theory of Dynamic Team Leadership." In *Team Effectiveness in Complex Organisations: Cross-Disciplinary Perspectives and Approaches (SIOP Frontier Series),* eds. E. Salas, G.F. Goodwin and C.S. Burke, 113–156. New York: Taylor and Francis.

Kram, K.E., and D.T. Hall. 1989. "Mentoring as an Antidote to Stress During Corporate Trauma." *Human Resource Management* 28, no. 4, pp. 493–510.

Kram, K.E., and M.C. Higgins. 2012. "A New Approach to Mentoring." *The Wall Street Journal.*

Kram, K.E., and L.A. Isabella. 1985. "Mentoring Alternatives: The Role of Peer Relationships in Career Development." *Academy of Management Journal* 28, no. 1, pp. 110–132.

Kuntz, J., and J. Gomes. 2012. "Transformational Change in Organisations: A Self-Regulation Approach." *Journal of Organizational Change Management* 25, no. 1, pp. 143–162.

Kyndt, E., F. Dochy, P. Onghena, and H. Baert. 2012. "The Learning Intentions of Low-Qualified Employees: A Multilevel Approach." *Adult Education Quarterly* 63, no. 2, pp. 165–189.

Lam, T.Y.M., September 2–3, 2010. "Managing the Growth of Social Housing Organisations." COBRA 2010 conference. The Construction, Building and Real Estate Research Conference of the Royal Institute of Chartered Surveyors, held at Dauphine Université, Paris.

Latta, G.F. 2009. "A Process of Organizational Change in Cultural Context (OC³ Model)." *Journal of Leadership & Organizational Studies* 16, no. 1, pp. 19–37.

Lee, S.Y.D., B.J. Weiner, M.I. Harrison, and C.M. Belden. 2013. "Organizational Transformation: A Systematic Review of Empirical Research in Health Care and Other Industries." *Medical Care Research and Review* 70, no. 2, pp. 115–142.

Leroy, F. 2002. "Socialization Processes During the Post-Merger Integration Phase: Conditions for Tacit Knowledge Sharing and Construction of Common Narratives." In *Third European Conference on Organizational Knowledge, Learning, and Capabilities, Greece.*

Lewin, K. 1951. *Field Theory in Social Science.* New York: Harper & Brothers.

Lord, P., M. Atkinson, and H. Mitchell. 2008. *Mentoring and Coaching for Professionals: A Study of the Research Evidence.* National Federation for Educational Research, UK.

Luecke, R., and H. Ibarra. 2004. *Coaching and Mentoring: How to Develop Top Talent and Achieve Stronger Performance.* New York: Harvard Business Review Press.

Malone. D., and J. Turner. 2010. "The Merger of AOL and Time Warner: A Case Study." *Journal of the International Academy for Case Studies* 16, no. 7, pp. 103–110.

Marks, M.L. 1997. "Consulting in Mergers and Acquisitions: Interventions Spawned by Recent Trends." *Journal of Organizational Change Management* 10, no. 3, pp. 267–279.

Marks, M.L., and P.H. Mirvis. 1997. "Revisiting the Merger Syndrome: Crisis Management." *Mergers and Acquisitions – Philadelphia* 32, no. 1, pp. 34–40.

Marks, M.L., and P.H. Mirvis. 2010. *Joining Forces: Making One Plus One Equal Three in Mergers, Acquisitions and Alliances.* San Francisco: Jossey-Bass.

Matsuo, M. 2018. "How does Managerial Coaching Affect Individual Learning? The Mediating Roles of Team and Individual Reflexivity." *Personnel Review.*

McClellan, J., K. Levitt, and G. DiClementi. 2017. "Emotional Intelligence and Positive Organizational Leadership: A Conceptual Model for Positive Emotional Influence." *Journal of Behavioral and Applied Management* 17, no. 3, p. 2626.

McKimm, J., C. Jollie, and M. Hatter. 2007. "Mentoring: Theory and Practice. Preparedness to Practice Project." Available from http://Londondeanry.ac.uk (accessed May 08, 2012).

Megginson, D., and D. Clutterbuck. 2005. "Creating a Coaching Culture." *Industrial and Commercial Training* 38, no. 5, pp. 232–237.

Mezirow, J. 1991. *Transformative Dimensions of Adult Learning.* San Francisco: Jossey-Bass.

Miao, C., R.H. Humphrey, and S. Qian. 2018. "Emotional Intelligence and Authentic Leadership: A Meta-Analysis." *Leadership & Organization Development Journal.*

Mirc, N. 2013. "Human Impacts on the Performance of Mergers and Acquisitions." In *Advances in Mergers and Acquisitions* eds. C. L. Cooper and S. Finkelstein, 1–31. Bingley: Emerald.

Mirvis, P.H., and M.L. Marks. 2003. *Managing the Merger: Making It Work.* Washington: Beard Books.

Morgeson, F.P., D.S. DeRue, and E.P. Karam. 2010. "Leadership in Teams: A Functional Approach to Understanding Leadership Structures and Processes." *Journal of Management* 36, no. 1, pp. 5–39.

Mulgan, G., and D. Albury. 2003. *Innovation in the Public Sector.* Strategy Unit, Cabinet Office, UK.

Nguyen, H., and B.H. Kleiner. 2003. "The Effective Management of Mergers." *Leadership & Organisational Development Journal* 24, no. 8, pp. 447–454.

Oliver, C., and P. Aggleton. 2002. "Mentoring for Professional Development in Health Promotion: A Review of Issues Raised by Recent Research." *Health Education* 102, no. 1, pp. 30–38.

Olivero, G., K.D. Bane, and R. Kopelman. 1997. "Executive Coaching as a Transfer of Training Tool: Effects on Productivity in a Public Agency." *Public Personnel Management* 26, 4, pp. 461–469.

Orenstein, R.L. 2007. *Multidimensional Executive Coaching.* New York: Springer.

Parsloe, E. 1995. *Coaching, Mentoring, and Assessing: A Practical Guide to Developing Competence.* New York: Kogan Page.

Patel, K. 2021. "10 Common Reasons Why Mergers and Acquisitions Fail." *DealRoom,* https://dealroom.net/blog/reasons-why-mergers-and-acquisitions-fail (accessed March 20, 2021).

Patel, V.M., O. Warren, K. Ahmed, P. Humphris, S. Abbasi, H. Ashrafian, and T. Athanasiou. 2011. "How Can We Build Mentorship in Surgeons of the Future?" *ANZ Journal of Surgery* 81, no. 6, pp. 418–424.

Peterson, D.B. 2009. "Coaching and Performance Management: How Can Organisations Get the Greatest Value?" In *Performance Management: Putting Research into Action,* eds. J. W. Smither and M. London, 115–156. San Francisco: Wiley.

Pettigrew, A. 1987. "Context and Action in the Transformation of the Firm." *Journal of Management Studies* 24, no. 6, 649–670.

Portnoy, S. 2006. "Divorce coaches: A New Resource for Matrimonial Lawyers." *American Journal of Family Law* 19, no. 4, pp. 231–235.

Puranam, P., H. Singh, and S. Chaudhuri. 2009. "Integrating Acquired Capabilities: When Structural Integration is (Un)Necessary." *Organization Science* 20, no. 2, pp. 313–328.

Rafferty, A.E., and M.A. Griffin. 2006. "Perceptions of Organizational Change: A Stress and Coping Perspective." *Journal of Applied Psychology* 91, no. 5, pp. 1154–1162.

Ragins, B.R., and K.E. Kram. 2007. "The Roots and Meaning of Mentoring." In *The Handbook of Mentoring at Work: Theory, Research and Practice, eds.* B.R. Ragins and K. E. Kram, 3–15. Thousand Oaks, CA: Sage.

Ralfe, J. 2010. "Change is a Constant Requiring a Coach." *Library Management* 31. nos. 4/5 291–303.

Renneboog, L., and C. Vansteenkiste. 2019. "Failure and Success in Mergers and Acquisitions." *Journal of Corporate Finance* 58, pp. 650–699.

Richardson, P. 2004. *The Life Coach: Become the Person You've Always Wanted to Be.* London: Hamlyn.

Rigsby, J.T., P.H. Siegel, and P.D. Spiceland. 1998. "Mentoring Among Management Advisory Services Professionals: An Adaptive Mechanism to Cope with Rapid Corporate Change." *Managerial Auditing Journal* 13, no. 2, pp. 107–116.

Risley, K., and H. Cooper. 2011. "Professional Coaching: An Innovative and Promising Leadership Development and Career Enhancement Approach for Public Health Professionals." *Health Promotion Practice* 12, no. 4, pp. 497–501.

Robinson-Walker, C. 2012. "Coaching Comes of Age." *Nurse Leader* 10, no. 2, pp. 12–13.

Rogers, J. 2012. *Facilitating Reflective Learning: Coaching, Mentoring & Supervision,* 2nd ed. London: Kogan Page.

Rossi, D.M. 2010. "Learning Relationships in Online Contexts: A Substantive Theory Constructed From the Integrated Analyses of Learner–Learner Interaction and Knowledge Construction in an Undergraduate Communication Course." [PhD Thesis.] University of Southern Queensland, Australia.

Sarala, R.M., E. Vaara, and P. Junni. 2019. "Beyond Merger Syndrome and Cultural Differences: New Avenues for Research on the "Human Side" of Global Mergers and Acquisitions (M&As)." *Journal of World Business* 54, no. 4, pp. 307–321.

Seo, M., and N.S. Hill. 2005. "Understanding the Human Side of Merger and Acquisition: An Integrative Framework." *Journal of Applied Behavioural Science* 41, no. 4, pp. 422–443.

Siegel, P.H. 2000. "Using Peer Mentoring During Periods of Uncertainty." *Leadership and Organisation Development Journal* 21, no. 5, pp. 243–253.

Smither, J., M. London, R. Flautt, Y. Vargas, and I. Kucine. 2003. "Can Working With an Executive Coach Improve Multisource Feedback Rating Overtime? A Quasi-Experimental Field Study." *Personnel Psychology* 56, no. 1, pp. 23–44.

Smither, J., and M. London. 2009. "Best Practice in Performance Management." In *Performance Management: Putting Research Into Action*, eds. J. Smither and M. London, 585–625. San Francisco: Jossey-Bass.

Smolska, M., 2019. "Team Coaching as a Tool to Improve Team Performance." *Scientific Journal of the Military University of Land Forces* 51.

Tajfel, H. 1972. "Social categorization. English manuscript of 'La catégorisation sociale'." In ed. S. Moscovici, *Introduction à la Psychologie Sociale*, 272–302. Paris: Larousse.

Tajfel, H., and J.C. Turner. 1979. "An Integrative Theory of Social Conflict." In *The Social Psychology of Intergroup Relations*, eds. W.G. Austin and S. Worchel, 7–24. California: Brooks/Cole

Terry, D.J. 2001. "Intergroup Relations and Organizational Mergers." In *Social Identity Processes in Organizational Contexts*, eds. M.A. Hogg and D.J. Terry, 229–247. Philadelphia, PA: Psychology Press.

Thorwid, H., and N. Vinge. 2020. "Organizational Culture and its Implications on Post-Acquisition Integration: A Case Study of a Merger Between Two Entrepreneurial Firms."

Thurston, P.W., C.P. D'Abate, and E.R. Eddy. 2012. "Mentoring as an HRD Approach: Effects on Employee Attitudes and Contributions Independent of Core Self-Evaluation." *Human Resource Development Quarterly* 23, no. 2, pp. 139–165.

Toit, A.D. 2007. "Making Sense Through Coaching." *Journal of Management Development* 26, no. 3, pp. 282–291.

Tosey, P., and G. Robinson. 2002. "When Change Is No Longer Enough: What Do We Mean By 'Transformation' In Organizational Change Work?" *The TQM Magazine* 14, no. 2, pp. 100–109.

Trenner, L. 2013. "Business Coaching for Information Professionals: Why It Offers Such Good Value for Money in Today's Economic Climate." *Business Information Review* 30, no. 1, pp. 27–34.

Ullrich, J., and D.R. Van Dick. 2007. "The Group Psychology of Mergers & Acquisitions: Lessons From the Social Identity Approach." In *Advances in Mergers and Acquisitions,* eds. C.L. Cooper and G. Finkelstein, 1–15. Amsterdam: JAI Press.

Vakola, M., and I. Nikolaou. 2005. "Attitudes Towards Organizational Change: What Is the Role of Employees' Stress And Commitment?" *Employee Relations* 27, no. 2, pp. 160–174.

Van Dick, R. 2004. "My Job Is My Castle: Identification in Organizational Contexts." In *International Review of Industrial and Organizational Psychology,* eds. C. L. Cooper and I. T. Robertson, 171–203. Chichester: Wiley.

Verma, Y. September 12, 2019. "Never Should Have Happened: Acquisition Narrative of Sprint and Nextel." *Inventiva,* Available at www.inventiva.co.in/stories/yamini/never-should-have-happened-acquisition-narrative-of-sprint-and-nextel/ (accessed January 10, 2021).

Wales, S. 2003. "Why Coaching?" *Journal of Change Management* 3, no. 3, pp. 275–282.

Ward, C., and D. Preece. 2012. "Leadership Development: For the '*here*' and the '*now*'. 13th International Conference on Human Resource Development Research and Practice across Europe, 23–25 May 2012: The future of HRD – 2020 and beyond: Challenges and Opportunities. University of Lusiada de Famalicao, Portugal.

Wasylyshyn, K. 2003. "Executive Coaching: An Outcome Study. *Consulting Psychology Journal: Practice and Research* 55, no. 2, pp. 94–106.

Wasylyshyn, K., B. Gronsky, and J. Hass. 2006. "Tigers, Stripes, and Behaviour Change: Survey Results of a Commissioned Coaching Programme." *Consulting Psychology Journal: Practice and Research* 58, no. 2, pp. 65–81.

Weber, R.A., and C.F. Camerer. 2003. "Cultural Conflict and Merger Failure: An Experimental Approach." *Management Science* 49, no. 4, pp. 400–415.

Weston, J.F., and S.C. Weaver. 2001. *Mergers & Acquisitions.* New York: McGraw-Hill.

William, W.L. 2005. *The Impact of a Recent Merger Between Two Aerospace Companies on the Resulting Organisational Culture on the Newly Formed Entity.* ProQuest Information and Learning Company. E-theses, University of Hong Kong, China.

Worral, L., C.L. Cooper, and F. Campbell-Jamison. 1998. "The Impact of Organisational Change on the Work Experiences and Perceptions of Public Sector Managers." *Personnel Review* 29, no. 5, pp. 613–636.

Yetton, P., S. Henningsson, and N. Bjorn-Andersen. 2013. "'Ready to Acquire': IT Resources for a Growth-By-Acquisition Strategy." *MIS Quarterly Executive* 12, no. 1, pp. 19–35.

Zachary, L.J. 2005. *Creating a Mentoring Culture: The Organisation's Guide*. San Francisco: Jossey-Bass.

Zeus, P., and S. Skiffington. 2000. *The Complete Guide to Coaching at Work*. Roseville, NSW: McGraw-Hill.

Zeus, P., and S. Skiffington. 2005. *The Coaching at Work Toolkit: A Complete Guide to Techniques and Practices*. Sydney: McGraw-Hill.

About the Author

Dr. Muhammad Rafique is a chartered accountant, management consultant, executive coach, and an educationalist. Dr. Rafique is an assistant professor at Nottingham University and course director for MSc accounting and finance. He provided accountancy, taxation, and business consultancy advice to various organizations in private and public sectors, including McCann, HSBC, Audit Commission, and National Health Service. He has special interest in transformational change and corporate governance and has served as board member for various organizations.

Index

OTHER TITLES IN THE FINANCE AND FINANCIAL MANAGEMENT COLLECTION

John Doukas, Old Dominion University, Editor

- *Understanding the Financial Industry Through Linguistics* by Richard C. Robinson
- *Understanding Cryptocurrencies* by Ariel Santos-Alborna
- *Sustainable Finance and Impact Investing* by Alan S. Gutterman
- *The Non-Timing Trading System* by George O. Head
- *Small Business Finance and Valuation* by Rick Nason and Dan Nordqvist
- *Finance for Non-Finance Executives* by Anurag Singal
- *Blockchain Hurricane* by Kate Baucherel
- *Risk Management for Nonprofit Organizations* by Rick Nason and Omer Livvarcin
- *Conservative Options Trading* by Michael C. Thomsett
- *Understanding Behavioral BIA$* by Daniel C. Krawczyk and George H. Baxter
- *Valuation of Indian Life Insurance Companies* by Prasanna Rajesh
- *Understanding Momentum in Investment Technical Analysis* by Micheal C. Thomsett

Concise and Applied Business Books

The Collection listed above is one of 30 business subject collections that Business Expert Press has grown to make BEP a premiere publisher of print and digital books. Our concise and applied books are for...

- Professionals and Practitioners
- Faculty who adopt our books for courses
- Librarians who know that BEP's Digital Libraries are a unique way to offer students ebooks to download, not restricted with any digital rights management
- Executive Training Course Leaders
- Business Seminar Organizers

Business Expert Press books are for anyone who needs to dig deeper on business ideas, goals, and solutions to everyday problems. Whether one print book, one ebook, or buying a digital library of 110 ebooks, we remain the affordable and smart way to be business smart. For more information, please visit www.businessexpertpress.com, or contact sales@businessexpertpress.com.

www.ingramcontent.com/pod-product-compliance
Lightning Source LLC
Chambersburg PA
CBHW061750270326
41928CB00011B/2447